LIVING with kids

ideas and solutions for family-friendly interiors

GLOUCESTER MASSACHUSETTS

ROCKPORT PUBLISHERS

EUGENIA SANTIESTEBAN

First published in the United States of America by
Rockport Publishers, Inc.
33 Commercial Street
Gloucester, Massachusetts 01930-5089
Telephone: (978) 282-9590
Fax: (978) 283-2742
www.rockpub.com

Library of Congress Cataloging-in-Publication Data

Santiesteban, Eugenia.
 Living with kids: ideas for family-friendly interiors / Eugenia
Santiesteban.
   p. cm.
 ISBN 1-56496-966-5
 1. Children's rooms. 2. Interior decoration. I. Title.
NK2117.C4 S26 2003
747.7'7—dc21   2002153216

ISBN 1-56496-966-5

10 9 8 7 6 5 4 3 2 1

Design: Peter King & Company
Cover Image: ©Paul Massey/Living Etc./IPC Syndication
Endpaper pattern, Kira Kira. courtesy of Marimekko
Copyeditor: Stacey Ann Follin
The publisher wishes to extend special thanks to Dorothy Williams
for her terrific finesse with the manuscript.

Printed in China

To my family—for all your support and especially, your unconditional love.

contents

living
with kids

ABOVE *Today's hardworking parents want to spend their leisure hours enjoying the company of their children, rather than doing housekeeping. Sturdy but comfortable wooden furniture, washable slipcovers, and easy-to-clean surfaces help make this possible.*

Gone are the days of formal sitting rooms where children were seen and not heard. In today's homes, families work and play together in the same spaces. Children are the center of the household, and every inch of space should be designed to accommodate the wear and tear that goes along with family living.

But this doesn't mean you have to sacrifice beauty for comfort. Family oriented and still chic? You can raise your family in style—and it's a lot easier than you might think! The options are endless, and in this book, you'll explore all the ways in which you can create a home that is as sturdy and safe as it is beautiful. You'll learn to plan for both the short and long term, designing livable, efficient, and, yes, timeless rooms that will expand and adapt to your family's needs as they change over time.

Within these pages you'll find inspired yet practical ideas for every room of the house, as well as solutions for problem areas. From living rooms to mudrooms, *Living with Kids* examines every angle in functional, stylish family living. Whether you're welcoming your first baby or making room for a growing clan, you'll find the advice you need here. Each chapter includes tips on shopping for furniture and kid-friendly materials, tips and tricks for organizing spaces, and style suggestions.

Most important, you'll learn to put aside the usual rules and regulations of decorating. Designing a home with children in mind should be fun. Be practical, but a bit irreverent. Inspiration can come from anywhere—perhaps most notably from your children themselves. Their input is invaluable, especially in places they call their own. Approach the delicious task of creating a beautiful home as a fun-filled activity for the entire family. They will love you for it. That's what this book is all about—living with kids, and loving it.

introduction

ground rules for family-friendly design

As you proceed, it is helpful to keep certain guidelines in mind. For example, choose furniture that you not only love but that is also practical. Always try to buy well-made furniture: It will better stand up to heavy use and perhaps even become an heirloom that you pass on to your child. Sturdier woods such as oak and mahogany are less ubiquitous than they used to be, but they'll last a lifetime. Well-constructed pine or other lighter woods can serve just as well.

Furniture commonly outlasts its original use and usually can be reassigned elsewhere or adapted to fit a family's changing needs, so buy with long-term plans in mind. If you buy things you really love, you'll be more likely to want to use them again and again. Remember: Growing children have quickly changing needs, which means frequent rearranging of furniture from room to room.

Designing kid-friendly spaces might also mean shrinking away from placing delicate family heirlooms in high-traffic areas like the living room; these pieces can be reassigned as well. Your great aunt's Wedgwood vase might really look great in the guest room. Don't hide away all your antiques though, especially the less-delicate ones. It's never too early to teach children to be respectful of possessions.

Organization and appropriate storage are key. Families accumulate clutter. Your home will look and work better if you figure out where and when the clutter accumulates, and design your home so that intercepting it is easier. Cubbies for soccer cleats in the mudroom, a rack for kids' computer game discs in the office by the computer—coming up with creative solutions is better than forever picking up the piles.

Remember that inspiration can come from anywhere. Be sure to keep yourself open to ideas you might incorporate into your decorating scheme. Whether it's a bedroom layout spotted at your next-door neighbors' home, or the cerulean blue of the ceiling at Grand Central Station, all is fodder for decorating. Don't discriminate; just remember those ideas that appeal to you and apply them in your space. You'll be surprised at the end result.

1 GETTING started

Now that you've decided to redo your home, the first step is outlining your goals. Whether you're planning a complete renovation, or just some minor streamlining and beautifying, writing your ideas down will help you get organized. Start with a comprehensive wish list. Write down everything you'd like to do, and then prioritize. Which things on your list are most important and most achievable? Do a little research at this point. What do things really cost? Talk to friends who have survived renovations or whose homes you admire, and ask them what works and what doesn't. Think about the alternatives: Can you paint or resurface your existing kitchen cupboards, or are new ones necessary?

Once you've decided on the targets and goals of your project, go over your plans with all the members of your family. Asking for help and ideas is a great way to get kids involved in a project. After all, everyone in the household should have a say, and if it's something directly involving their lives and day-to-day routine, you'll be surprised at how much input children will want to add!

OPPOSITE Before you start any redesign of your home, gather the family to discuss their needs and preferences so you can design a home that accommodates everyone. Conversation, board games, television, or video games can take place simultaneously in this family's living room.

the budget

Once everyone in the family has approved the overall plan, the next step is creating a budget and an action plan. Depending on the size of your renovation, the money that you'll need to set aside for your project will differ greatly. If you plan on making major changes, it may be helpful to get professional estimates. If so, obtain quotes from at least a few different professionals to ensure that you're getting a fair price. Estimates can vary widely. Use a spreadsheet to get organized and put all budget information in one easily accessible place.

Consider Your Timetable

Next, make a list of the rooms that you want to make less-extensive changes to. Estimate the costs for each, including paint jobs, furniture, storage systems, and accessories. If replacing furniture is too costly, new slipcovers, upholstery, or even new bedding can completely change the look of a room without the hefty price tag. It's also important to make a long-term plan. How long will the changes that you make need to last? Are you in a rental apartment and planning to move within a few years, or are you in a house and expecting to live there for decades? Whether your budget is limited, or you want to plan for the long haul, trendy options are better left to accessories and smaller objects than to large pieces of furniture. Versatility can be key in such cases.

Once you've talked to the contractors or workmen you'll need to hire, you should discuss the renovation schedule with the rest of the family. Maybe it's best to work on the children's rooms over the summer while they're away at camp or busy with summer activities, rather than in the fall when they're just getting back into school. Or perhaps fall is a good time to work on the living room when everyone is gone much of the day because of work or school. Decide what works best for you and your family and try to come up with a realistic time frame.

Remember that it isn't necessary to get everything done all at once, especially when buying expensive pieces of furniture. Even for renovation, accomplishing a little bit at a time over a longer time span might be better if you're making costly changes. Or perhaps if the budget isn't an issue, you'd like to get the work done or make all purchases you need as quickly as possible to disrupt your family as little as possible. Decorating is never really done. Improvements can always be made, but the key is to stick to your budget and know when to stop. Otherwise, your finances can easily spiral out of control.

OPPOSITE Is the ideal summer beach house always in your dreams? Use elements of the sea and other nautical keepsakes—seashells, buoys, blue and white stripes—to evoke the feeling of sun, sand, and carefree laughter.

picking a design aesthetic

Next, get inspired! Rip pages that you like out of magazines or catalogs. If you admire a home or a room that you've seen, jot down notes about it. Collect swatches of fabric that catch your eye, or paint-color chips that you're considering. As with anything, inspiration can come from anywhere—a decorating magazine, the lighting in a museum, or a display window that catches your eye as you walk down the street. And never be afraid to borrow. If a room you've been in feels comfortable, it's perfectly acceptable to mimic the layout or color scheme in your own home. Start keeping a folder with all the ideas you collect. It will be a reference when you're feeling stuck, and a place to gather your inspirations. You'll be surprised at how many images and samples you collect—and you'll be gratified when you look back and see how you translated those ideas into reality.

It is helpful at this point to narrow down your style preferences. Look at your favorite rooms and try to figure out which style category they fall into: classic American colonial, French country, modern, fifties retro, Swedish country—almost any look can be translated into a comfortable, beautiful family home. It's OK to be eclectic too, but it's better to mix and match on purpose than by accident. Serendipity notwithstanding, you'll save time and effort if you focus your search before you start.

Use What You've Got

Location often decides decorating needs as well. How much light does the room get, and which way does it face? Does it have a view—of a lake, ocean, rugged mountains, or city rooftops—that you want to emphasize? If the house is in a city, should you soundproof the baby's room? Who will use rooms the most, and for what purposes? All these factors should influence your decisions. Consider the design elements you already have in the house, especially architectural details. High ceilings give a wonderfully majestic feel to a room, besides providing an amazing backdrop for art. Existing fireplaces, mantelpieces, or columns have an air of built-in *gravitas*. Beams, moldings, and other structures can give character to a room. If details such as these aren't already in your home, some of them can be added or mimicked. For example, wainscoting is fairly easy to add to a bedroom or bathroom and it lends an old-fashioned, country feeling to a room. Your interior decoration doesn't have to conform to the style of your house, but considering its architecture beforehand will help define what you need to do.

Choose the Right Paint

The color of a room also influences the decor. A good way to decide which colors you want is to buy several options in a tester size; many paint companies sell small vials for such a purpose. Paint poster boards with the different hues and hang them up on the wall in the room you'll be painting. The nuances in paint formulas are surprisingly different from one another, as is the way in which colors look in a specific room, depending on the quantity and quality of light the room gets.

OPPOSITE Never underestimate the power of color to transform a room. Set off a strong shade, like that of these walls and bed, against a stark white background—linens and woodwork in this case—for an effect that's pure magic.

input from the family

Don't forget about who will be living in the rooms. Including children in the planning process not only helps them feel invested in the outcome but also provides refreshing ideas that reflect the children's personalities, and gives them an opportunity to mark their own territory, especially in their bedrooms. Set boundaries, however. Your children may want to poster their room with magazine pages, or hope to have a tent in the middle of the room for a bed, but that doesn't mean you're obliged to comply. (It's never too early to teach them the value of practicality!) As long as you allow them a voice in making choices, they'll feel more in control of their space. If, for example, you're set on buying a particular bed for your child, let the child choose the bedding. Even if you don't love the choices the child makes, you can repaint and redecorate the room later. In the end, the important thing is that your child will remember that you listened.

survival tips

Although planning a renovation project can be fun if you involve your children, in reality, it can be long and complicated and create lots of tension within a family. The schedule lags behind, expenses multiply, and differences can become a source of struggle. Understand that problems can arise, and be prepared to deal with them as they come.

If you're on a strict schedule—for example, renovating a bedroom to prepare for a new baby—have a backup plan in case something goes awry. Maybe another room in the house, or even a cradle in the master bedroom, can serve as a temporary nursery until the real room is ready. A renovation is an evolving, constantly changing process. You may run into construction snags that you couldn't have foreseen, or you may find yourself changing your

mind a few times during the process, or not liking something once it's done. It's always better to try and change something you don't love at the initial stages rather than five years down the road.

Before construction starts, have a conversation with your family, letting them know how long you expect the process to take, as well as the extent of the changes. Ask for their patience and cooperation. If sacrifices must be made, try to help the children remember that maturity is appreciated, and that the long-term result will be worth waiting for. Remind yourself that the whole point of the renovation is to make a more relaxed, comfortable home for your family.

OPPOSITE Work together with your child to arrive at a compromise. Maybe putting toys on the kitchen floor isn't the best idea, but don't rule it out before you give it a try! If your floor is less spacious than this, perhaps a bin for crayons, paper, and scissors on the kitchen table can provide another way to bring toys into the kitchen.

2 KITCHENS

Varying in size, style, and purpose, the kitchen is
often considered the linchpin of the house. From
the centuries-old image of a crackling hearth that
drew family members to the belly of the house to
the modern-day snacking stop and message center,
the kitchen remains as a primetime space for
everyone. Whether you're cooking, entertaining,
or just simply eating, it's likely that a family-friendly
kitchen has requirements to fill such as safety,
storage, and function.

*RIGHT Draw your family together by making your kitchen
serve several functions at once—workstation, eating area, and
chef's quarters. Provide plenty of seating, like these wood-
and-stainless steel bar stools. Mix stainless-steel surfacing
with brick walls for a sophisticated yet warm effect. A small-
screen television discreetly perched above the refrigerator
serves its function without cluttering the kitchen work area.*

your kitchen's purpose

Food is literally sustenance for living and as such, brings families together, day after day. Whether it's a quick snack or an elaborate dinner, there's never a day that the kitchen isn't put to use. Food is love, or as M.F.K. Fisher said even more eloquently: "It seems to me that our three basic needs, for food and security and love, are so mixed and mingled and entwined that we cannot straightly think of one without the others. So it happens that when I write of hunger, I am really writing about love and the hunger for it." Naturally, a dark, unwelcoming kitchen is one of the first places that you would begin revamping for your family.

A well-organized kitchen doesn't necessarily mean top-of-the line appliances and all the amenities. As in any other room in the house, the ideal decor is what works best for you and your family. Stainless steel and bleached wood are both attractive and modern, but stylish kitchens come in every variety. Colorful wood, lots of tchotchkes, and mismatched place mats work just as well for streamlined living, as long as the kitchen is well organized. If you're an accomplished chef, it's probably necessary for you to have high-quality machinery and utensils. But if you're strictly cooking the most elementary basics, that's fine too; maybe the sparsest collection of pots and pans will suffice. Anything goes.

Because the kitchen often doubles as a dining area, it may also be important to consider which meals are served there. If only breakfast and snacks are consumed in the kitchen, an informal daytime decor serves the purpose. If dinner in the kitchen is a regular habit, you may want to consider a more versatile style that transforms easily from a casual lunch spot to a serene setting for evening dining for the entire family, as well as a guest or two. For instance, you'll want to fit in a table and chairs rather than just stools at a counter, and shades rather than bare windows will make the kitchen feel cozier at night.

If your kitchen opens onto the living room and transforms into a party room when you entertain, a kitchen island can do double duty as a bar for serving cocktails, and still be childproof and safe for the children to roam around during the day. If you entertain often, you may want to consider putting in an extra oven, an extra-large refrigerator, and lots of storage areas, because advance preparation is key to managing a dinner party and family life at the same time.

OPPOSITE *Although kitchens aren't normally play areas, the occasional scoot-by is allowed en route to the outdoor patio of this house. Place crystal vases and bowls out of reach but visible to add a glamorous effect. A farmhouse-style wooden table paired with sturdy, functional modern chairs immediately makes this kitchen a comfortable place for family dining or casual entertaining.*

ORGANIZING: design basics

Creating order in the kitchen seems like making method out of madness in some cases, but a well-organized kitchen can transform the cooking experience from chaos to pleasure. Use your space creatively. Whether you have a pantry or just a few cabinets, you'll be surprised at how much mileage you can get out of your storage space.

Even the smallest and most mundane spaces can serve as storage room. Pretty vases, bowls, or glass can be stored atop cabinets that don't reach all the way to the ceiling. Kitchen islands or butcher blocks with a lower tier can hold items too, as long as they aren't items that would be dangerous to children. Make sure no space is left unturned. Sometimes additional shelving can be added to existing cabinets to increase surface space. Faux drawers under the sink can even be transformed into a shallow, pivoting drawer to hold a sponge or utensils. Cabinets with shelves that slide out can keep cookware, especially stacked pots and pans or baking dishes, easily accessible. If you don't already have a cabinet over the refrigerator, consider adding one.

PANTRY POLISH

- Store food or other objects in an interesting way—in empty mason jars or other glass vessels.
- Add overhead pot racks to free up valuable storage space and make the kitchen more attractive, especially if you have polished copper pots.
- Store frequently used utensils in easy-to-reach jars to free up storage space elsewhere.
- Use the often-forgotten under-sink area, too!
- Look for inefficiently used spaces where you could add shelves, racks, or drawers.
- Install glass cabinets in the kitchen so the whole family can find things easily. Even young kids can fix themselves breakfast if you keep cereal, bowls, and spoons on the lower shelves in those cabinets.
- Don't forget to add a message board: The kitchen is often the family's communication center.

OPPOSITE A versatile, chrome storage rack like this one can be placed along a wall to increase pantry space. The butcher block on top of the smaller rack adds an extra work surface too. If your rack has wheels, make sure they lock in place so that children can't move it when they're playing.

the family-friendly kitchen

No matter the size, shape, or design, every family kitchen must have a common denominator, and that is safety. It's important for children to be aware of safety precautions and to learn rudimentary kitchen no-nos. And when decorating, it's important for you to consider safety details such as flooring that isn't too slick, tables with rounded corners, and surfaces that are durable enough for kids to use. Some safety considerations are obvious, like keeping knives and cleaning liquids out of the reach of toddlers, but look through your pediatrician's

child-proofing guidelines as you design your kitchen to be sure you don't overlook anything.

Ideally, the kitchen shouldn't double as a playroom, but the irresistible charm of baking cookies draws everyone in the house into the kitchen. And who minds having company in the kitchen? Just make sure you can navigate with ease and without tripping over toys. Again, the key to a kitchen that can successfully hold the entire family lies in its safety and organization.

OPPOSITE For a workstation that doubles as a seating area, use an extended kitchen island like this one, where cheerful yellow stools provide easy seating for baking cookies or conversation. For children's stools, make sure they're set off at the corner, away from dangerous appliances.

ABOVE For added storage, line shelves and drawers up an entire wall, like those in this whitewashed kitchen. Fragile glasses and containers are placed on high shelves, and durable books and bowls are within everyone's reach. Floral plates are hung on the wall to add a delicate touch, and an expandable, white-painted kitchen table gives a bit of practical savoir faire.

Carve Out Cooking and Eating Areas

A safe kitchen can still be stylish and comfortable. Farmhouse-style kitchen furnishings, built with durability in mind, can work in numerous hues and settings. If your taste runs more to modern style, stainless steel and stone can be made warmer with a few splashes of color. Stylish details can add flair to any kitchen, either sparingly or boldly.

The goal of making the kitchen a family-friendly spot can be helped by separating cooking and eating areas. Besides providing a built-in spot for impromptu dining, a kitchen island also gives the chef valuable work space; just remember to keep seats away from the stove and knives and cutting boards away from the seating area. If there's room, an informal table is one of the best ways to accommodate family time in the kitchen. It's also lovely to have an armchair or sofa in the kitchen to encourage family members to lounge while you cook. If you have small children, try to avoid using upholstered chairs at the table—keeping them clean is a hopeless task. If your dining room is on the formal side, have fun with the kitchen eating area. Bright colors look great and feel welcoming to children; let loose a little with bright, eye-popping hues, or, if you prefer, stick to a toned-down palette to encourage order and calm.

ABOVE Add friendly jolts of color to the kitchen with a window-seat bench outfitted with a striped cushion and loads of colorful pillows. For added effect, paint only a border or trim, like these cobalt-blue window frames that contrast with the wooden chairs and white furniture and add definition to the room.

KID-FRIENDLY: heavy-duty surfaces

Kitchen surfaces inevitably take lots of abuse, which is why they should be durable above all. Fortunately, many options are available, so kitchen surfaces can be resilient, family-friendly, and stylish all at once. By changing these surfaces, you can also update the entire look of your kitchen. Materials vary widely in price, however. Try to strike a balance between the best-looking, most functional, and most durable surface of your dreams and the right price.

STAINLESS STEEL

Stainless steel combines gleaming looks and professional-quality utilitarianism. Previously, it was used primarily in commercial kitchens, but its stark look can be softened by using wood for cabinets or furniture and by adding other homey details. Not only does it look polished, stainless steel is also extremely resilient. Stainless steel never stains or burns, making it a perfect child-safe surface in that respect. However, it does require constant cleaning—fingerprints are forever visible if it isn't pristine. But beware of the cost—it's an expensive material.

ABOVE For a coolly sharp kitchen that's still soft, consider wood. In this kitchen—with ceilings, cabinets, and a low kitchen table made of wood—a saunalike effect is created. The textured warmth of the wood softens the sleek, modern look, and the low benches lend a welcoming feel, inviting children to slide in. The backsplash tiles and linoleum work surfaces add a touch of practicality, as they are both washable and durable.

CORIAN SOLID SURFACES

Corian, a trademarked composite made by DuPont, is a technologically advanced surface material made of resins and minerals that can be shaped into any surface. Cuts or scratches can be sanded down like a wood surface, and it's extremely easy to maintain. The range of colors offered is extensive. Colors like apple green or intense blue-lavender are sure to make any kitchen pop. More conservative granite or marbled looks can be had if your taste runs on the quieter side.

CERAMIC SURFACES

Ceramic tiles are another alternative, and they come in a multitude of colors, sizes, and patterns. Unlike monochromatic stainless seal or Corian surfaces, tiles allow the option of creating a decorative pattern. Pick tiles within the same color family to give surfaces a weathered, imperfect look, or put together a rainbow of colors if you prefer a colorful, offbeat aesthetic. With tiles you can get more creative. They can also be finished with a paint sealant to protect them and make them easier to clean. Although tiles are resilient, be careful while chopping because even the strongest tiles can chip.

NATURAL MATERIALS

Natural materials such as wood, granite, or marble can make attractive surface materials, but as a whole, they're a bit more fragile. Wood surfaces naturally change over time, becoming weathered and scratched through everyday wear. But wood can also be treated with sealant to make it more durable, and it may fit the style and decor that you're aiming for. Granite and marble (like slate, limestone, and other stone tops) are much more resistant to scratches, but they are susceptible to stains. Unlike wood, they can't be sanded down and may be bit more fragile if used in large sheets.

HEAVY-DUTY SURFACES

- Flooring and surfaces should be stylish but not too slippery; make sure your children can navigate easily.

- Consider the costs of all the options; they can differ dramatically.

- Realistically assess your kitchen use before deciding; the needs of a professional chef are different from those of an average household cook.

- Whether you opt for metal, marble, or wood, each can completely alter the look of your kitchen; therefore, once you choose the surface that best meets your needs, keep to your color palette for a more cohesive look.

- Easy-to-clean surfaces are a must in a high-activity kitchen. When children are around, countertops, floors, walls, chairs, and tables will all need frequent scrubbing. Avoid white floors.

- Add color on the counters or the floors if you want dramatic results.

ABOVE Although the actual kitchen in this house can fit only a small, round table, the dining nook alongside holds a wide, solid table that accommodates everything from a big family dinner to art projects. The zinc sheeting in the middle of the table can take much abuse, and the roomy benches had a prior life as church pews.

Make the Most of Awkward or Small Spaces

Although big, roomy kitchens are wonderful, in cities and smaller vacation homes in particular, kitchens are often compressed into one small space in which appliances, dishes, foodstuffs, and all the accoutrements of cooking must fit. When thinking small, don't also think dull and utilitarian. Small kitchens can still be welcoming family spaces with bright colors and accents, and proximity to comfortable seating. Additional storage like an armoire in the dining area can accommodate cooking utensils. If the space is seriously tiny and lacking in sunlight, consider opening it up to the rest of the house. Knocking down a wall can drastically improve the appearance of the room—as well as broadcast to the family that this space is not only for eating but also for relaxing.

In loft spaces where the kitchen is already just a nook off of the living room, there's no need to demolish any walls, but perhaps you want to section off the kitchen into its own area. Solution? Paint that area its own color, or mark the beginning of the kitchen with a large cabinet or other piece of furniture. Or, if you want to keep the room monochromatic, you can use screens to create room divisions, which, as a bonus, provide a place to pin up your children's artwork. It's also possible that simply the placement of the kitchen's appliances and furniture can provide enough separation.

Space restrictions shouldn't put a limit on your style. With a bit of ingenuity, a small space can get lots of mileage. Judicious use of color and thoughtful use of space can transform any kitchen from the purely functional into a family-ready, central location where meals can be prepared, homework can be done, and cookies can be baked.

ABOVE In this vacation-house duplex, the kitchen's open plan gives the illusion of a larger space. As a result, the counter bar with bar chairs becomes a gathering place for the family. The glass cabinets stock colorful dinnerware and decorative objects.

ABOVE To brighten up a small, dark kitchen, paint it taxicab yellow. Ordinary veneer cabinets with updated handles take on an altogether different look next to the cheery color. Brushed-aluminum lamps, fifties-style chairs, and the family's flea market finds help energize the space.

safety in a working kitchen

"The more, the merrier" is an adage that we've advocated for the kitchen, but how can all this fun be had while serious cooking takes place? Organization is the key to a viable kitchen that belongs to both chef and children. Although adults likely do most of the cooking in the kitchen, it shouldn't be considered an all-adult domain. Teach your children about kitchen safety. They should know what the different appliances are and any necessary safety precautions. If they're old enough to learn how to use some of the kitchen's devices, make sure they can use them properly and with caution. Careless accidents are common in the kitchen, but many are easily preventable. It's partic-ularly important to keep the paths clear between the major work spaces: stove, sink, refrigerator, and countertops. Make sure you can you get a pot of boiling water from stove to sink without having to negotiate obstacles. If you have toddlers and infants just learning to crawl and walk, consider setting up a safety zone. Use high chairs, safety gates, and playpens, and situate them away from appliances. Keep stools and chairs away from the stove so that inquisitive toddlers can't climb up.

Pots and pans must be easily accessible for a working chef. Hanging them on the wall or from the ceiling on a pot rack clears out lower cabinets and shelves and keeps heavy pots out of children's reach. Favorite utensils should be easily accessible. Pretty ceramics or jars can store spatulas, spoons, and ladles to help eliminate last-minute searches in a cluttered drawer. Knives can be hung on a wall, out of reach of small fingers. Some chefs like to display dry goods in glass containers. Pearly white rice grains, long strands of spaghetti, and viscous olive oil can look sculptural when displayed on a kitchen counter or in glass cabinets. Open counter space for chopping and food preparation is a must. Small appliances that are used often should also be kept close by.

OPPOSITE Put a storage unit next to your kitchen table so kids can do everything from artwork to board games while you cook; these things can be quickly swept away when dinner is ready. White paint, high ceilings, and brightly colored accents keep this kitchen area bright and welcoming, even without many windows.

SHOPPING: kid-safe appliances

When shopping for appliances, consider durability, style, and, of course, safety features. For ovens and ranges, make sure that they have not only safety locks but also adequate thermal insulation to prevent burns from occurring, should anyone accidentally brush up against them. Stove knobs shouldn't turn too easily or should be placed on the back of the stove top, rather than up front and low where little hands can easily reach them.

Microwave ovens are incredibly convenient for modern lifestyles, drastically reducing cooking and clean-up time. But for children, they can be a serious hazard because of their user-friendly accessibility. Make sure your microwave oven is inaccessible to young children and has safety-programming features.

In checking out the design of any appliance, make sure that children won't hurt themselves on sharp edges or be able to accidentally open something while leaning against it. Refrigerators should be especially difficult for toddlers to open. Cords should be hidden and out of reach, as well. Don't forget to cover all other visible outlets with plastic protectors.

Surfaces should be easy to clean. Although stainless steel looks fabulous, you'll have to work hard to keep fingerprints off. A slightly textured surface, like that used on many refrigerators, is a good alternative because it minimizes fingerprints, but it needs frequent cleaning to prevent it from looking grimy.

KITCHEN SAFETY

- Do a test run for safety when childproofing the kitchen; look at things from a child's perspective, and work from there.
- Set up a safety zone—that is, one where it's always OK for your child to stay.
- Place fragile items and dangerous appliances out of reach.
- Teach your child the rules of safety, but still remain vigilant.
- Check for safety features on all appliances and electrical equipment you buy.
- Style and design matter everywhere; once you've decided that something is safe, make sure it works with your decor.

OPPOSITE The look of appliances in a kitchen is as important to its appeal as any other detail. A gleaming, stainless-steel refrigerator and stove add glamour and provide a welcome contrast to the wood cabinets.

STYLE FILE: color palette

Kitchens can often benefit from a healthy dose of color. Whether you want bright, cheery walls or a muted, neutral background with a few colored appliances or pieces of furniture, any combination can work for your personal style and your family's needs. Adding some bright color gives your kitchen a friendly atmosphere. In compressed spaces, color can make a once-dull space interesting and lively.

Weathered or old furniture can be updated with a coat of shiny latex paint in fun colors like apple green, bright blue, or even stark white to contrast with colored accessories, and make the kitchen inviting to kids.

Color can be used creatively to evoke a particular atmosphere in the kitchen. Use your imagination to achieve the effect that you want, whether it's a fun hub of activity or a Zen-like sense of tranquillity. Color brings the look of a kitchen together, tying its practical functions together with its visual appeal. It underscores the notion that it is not only the working center of the house but also an informal welcoming space where the family gathers. Strong or bright tones can help blend in additional storage space or even make a compact space feel larger. If you don't paint the walls, small touches of color can also bring a distinct touch to a kitchen, whether it's one bright piece of furniture, like a table or countertop, or the addition of colorful accents throughout against a white or neutral-toned background. If you opt for a more muted look, subtle changes in tones can also give a kitchen a richer texture and make it more dramatic.

LEFT Paint cabinets in pastels, ranging from mint green to Pepto-Bismol pink for an off-beat but soft and inviting look in a kitchen short on space. In this one, lavender walls complete the playful aesthetic, while the kitchen table and chairs are kept in natural wood or neutral tones to keep from driving the look over the top, so people of all ages feel welcome.

OPPOSITE Add bright colors to make a room pop. These fuchsia-painted chairs pulled up to a table with a gingham table-cloth are set off against the whitewashed bead-board walls for a colorful yet fresh aesthetic in this kitchen's dining area.

COLOR PALETTE

- Choose your background color carefully. Whether you opt for a bright color or a neutral shade, keep in mind that the one you select may dictate the rest of the kitchen's decor.

- Avoid using flat paint in the kitchen; it won't wipe clean.

- If you have an open-plan kitchen, make sure the color goes well with the living room.

- If your kitchen has contrasting surfaces, be bold and make a statement with your color choice. Remember: These surfaces can balance the look of either a dramatic color or a stark white.

- To give the kitchen a special touch, add accents on the walls and especially in glassed-in cabinets. Consider decorative plates, beautiful stained glass, or whatever your whimsy.

- If you opt against lots of color with your paint choice, add splashes of it throughout with tablecloths, plates, and napkins.

- Don't forget window treatments. Beautiful solid fabrics or trendy toiles can add kick to any kitchen space. Of course, remember to keep the curtains away from any source of heat.

3 GATHERING places

If any room is the epicenter of the household, it's the living room. It's where the most time is logged, and where the majority of a family's activities take place. In the old-fashioned salon, conversation was always at its best. Often the star room of a house, it is a wonderful place that evokes memories of laughter, holiday gatherings, cocktail hours, and Sunday-morning downtime. However, it can also be the home's noisy crossroads—where homework is done, last-minute plans are made, and impromptu wrestling matches are decided. An overcrowded war room at its worst and a comfortable, utilitarian haven at its best, the living room must serve many purposes if it is to accomodate your family well.

OPPOSITE *A window seat is a great way to fill a window nook. With a custom-fit, upholstered cushion and a few soft pillows, a window seat can provide both a cozy reading area and extra seating for guests. The extra shelves underneath for storage are useful, too.*

designs that meet everyone's needs

To start, take all of the family's needs into consideration. What is your living room used for? Who uses it most? When do they use it? If these needs overlap, try to be creative about accommodating as many of them as possible. Can you create separate seating areas within the room? Can you give these seating areas separate light sources so the light level can be flexible for each? A couch and armchairs around a coffee table can occupy one end of the room and accommodate socializing, TV watching, and board games, while a table with chairs and a brighter overhead light sits at the other end and can be used for homework. Screens can partition off spaces from visual distraction. As a last resort, headphones can come in handy if, for instance, one child simply must watch a particular TV show while another needs to practice at the piano. It may take some careful thought, but with planning, multi-purpose living rooms can work.

LEFT Sleek, low sofas are paired with floor cushions for a relaxed attitude in this family's living room. A knotted-wool area rug leaves a comfortable play area, and high book-shelves display objects, photos, and books out of harm's way.

STYLE FILE: family photos

Photographs make a home your own by imbuing it with your family's own style and flair. Each photo keeps a loved one present or tells a story of a trip or holiday that your family spent together.

Black-and-white photographs blend seamlessly into any living room's decor. Vintage sepia-toned family photos and wedding portraits add meaning and a historical touch. Recent color photos of your children are always appropriate. Stylish details, like framing and placement, should be considered as carefully as any other element in the living room. Sterling-silver frames, painted rustic wood, or silver-gilt can give formal or fun touches to a living room without overdoing it. Various ready-made frames are available, as are flip-book stands and beautiful photo albums.

Photographs can be artfully arranged on a wall or clustered together in a cheerful crowd. They can be placed on a coffee table, propped on the shelf of a bookcase, or sprinkled judiciously in nooks around the living room. A few can sit atop a mantle, alongside other objects, such as candlesticks, a bud vase, or a collection of Murano glass. Or, if you prefer, you can devote an entire wall of the living room to family photographs that have been framed to dot the walls like art. Use the same-style frames for a unified look, and then group them together on the wall.

Arrange photos by theme or according to a specific time line. Create a small vignette by placing a photograph of a family trip to Europe next to an object acquired there. The vignette will tell a story every time it catches your eye. Group pictures of your children's graduations from kindergarten and grade school together, leaving room to add other photos in the future. Heirloom photographs, too, are a special way to display family history.

Your particular memories that have been so carefully recorded and preserved add a wonderful touch to a living room's style. Whether a tiny detail shot or a whole series of pictures from the latest family vacation, photographs can personalize the room in a unique way.

DISPLAYING FAMILY PHOTOGRAPHS

- Group photographs together on the wall above the sofa or mantel to make them the focal point of the room.
- Add souvenirs and vintage photos to a family room, as a way of keeping family history alive.
- Use black-and-white pictures for a monochromatic palette that seamlessly blends into a neutral decor.
- Hang photos at eye level, line them horizontally, or group them closely on one wall. There are no rules—go with whatever works best for you.
- Frames with interesting details can add glamour to a room without being extravagant. Choose frames made of silver, covered with leather, or wrapped in an exotic skin like alligator or shagreen.

the formal living room

Just as the living room is an important a place for family, it may also be the prime space for entertaining guests. However, sophisticated looks don't have to be stiff. Art and chic furniture can easily be mixed together for a living room that works for the entire family during the day, and transforms into an intimate setting for cocktails and conversation at night.

If your living room is the room for entertaining, it should be on the formal side. Keep in mind, however, it is possible to combine style with function. Sturdy twill is a good choice for covering sofas. It is resilient enough to withstand a lot of wear, and it can be easily washed, especially if it's in slipcover form. Another option that combines easy maintenance

with style is a woven floor treatment like a sisal or sea-grass rug. The natural textures are neutral enough to work in a variety of rooms and are no longer considered beach-house decor. They can be used in minimalist, pared-down rooms just as easily as in the most rococo of salons. Best of all, they are fairly inexpensive and durable, and they clean up easily with a good vacuum. An Oriental rug is another viable option for your floors. It can add a great deal of warmth and comfort underfoot, and if it is dark colored and patterned, it can hide a multitude of sins. Although you will want to stow away the heirloom rugs for when the kids are almost grown, a good-quality wool oriental is worth the investment.

BELOW To create a chic-yet-livable living room, cover a sofa in off-white twill, add colorful graphic pillows, and finish it off with a pair of funky, vintage armchairs. Black-and-white photographs on the wall add an elegant touch.

OPPOSITE In this living room, dark wood and velvet uphol-stery project a coolly sophisticated look against a canvas of neutral walls. Placing a traditional rug like this one in the center adds warmth and encourages flopping on the floor for games or reading.

Kid-friendly Formality

Creating a formal living room doesn't mean that kids can't feel at home there, too. Cotton and wool are good fabric choices for upholstered furniture because they are easy to clean (just be sure the fabric has been treated with a protective, stain-resistant coating), are sturdy enough to withstand trampoline practice every now and then when you aren't looking, and look good in any color. Keep in mind that both solid, light colors and solid, dark colors show spills and grime easily and are best avoided unless used as washable slipcovers. Leather is another good choice for upholstery because it is very durable and, unless it is the sleek modern black or beige variety, it will even gain character with wear and tear. Low tables of varying heights encourage activity and a casual atmosphere where sitting on the floor is allowed. Even if chic enough to host the most formal of gatherings, a room

doesn't have to scream, "Don't touch." Elements of warmth lend an inviting air—overstuffed cushions, roomy seating, soft throws, and a few plants create a comfortable atmosphere. A sprinkling of books never hurts, either.

Open space is essential for entertaining. It gives guests a chance to mingle and stretch their legs. However, ample seating is also important. Window seats along the corners of a living room provide extra spots that don't crowd floor space, double as separate reading nooks, and maintains the room's serious air.

Mantelpieces offer an opportunity to display something beautiful, whether it's a collection of china, jewel-toned Murano glass, or family photographs. Often serving as the focal point for a room, the mantelpiece is a place where you can showcase objects at a height safe from harm.

SHOPPING: sofas

Let's face it: Most of the time that your family spends in the living room is spent on the sofa. Whether for lounging and daydreaming, reading a novel, eating a light snack, or just watching television, the sofa is the most-used piece of furniture in the room. It needs to be comfortable, resilient, and attractive enough to serve as the room's centerpiece. Buying a sofa merits deliberation. The good news is that with so many options on the market, it shouldn't be difficult to choose the one that works best for your living room and lifestyle.

SOFA OPTIONS AND CONSIDERATIONS

When studying sofas, take note of dimensions. First of all, figure out the size of the biggest sofa that will fit in its allotted space. It's important that it not be dwarfed by a big space or dominate an area that's too small. And it must accommodate lots of family members all at once. For comfort, the depth and seat height of a sofa are key. Roomy sofas that can accommodate long legs—and even an entire family—are usually the deeper ones. But you may not want it so deep that you need a tow rope to climb out. Make sure you test drive before buying so your sofa is deep and tall enough for you and your family to be comfortable. Don't forget the necessity of soft cushions. Overstuffed sofas with lots of pillows and thick cushions also add a comfortable element. Realize that if you have young children, and you choose a sofa with a back made of separate pillows rather than one upholstered piece, the pillows may land on the floor frequently, usually to serve as a fort. If this bothers you, choose the more tailored, upholstered back. Details like the height of the back and the style of the arms are also important. Perhaps a high back might be too rigid for you; a low back might not seem cozy. You might prefer rounded or scrolled arms for a little extra padding, or more angular edges for a streamlined look. And it's worth it to pay a little more for firmer cushions. Foam cushions won't take the abuse children mete out. Pay attention to the details when searching for the ultimate sofa—they'll make a difference.

Fabric

Given all the activity it's expected to withstand, a sofa fabric should be strong to stand the test of time. Look for fabrics that are stain-resistant and washable, preferably by machine. A pristine, white sofa may look great at first, but it will require frequent cleaning. Opt for what's reasonable, low-maintenance, and still attractive. Keep in mind that lighter colors and solid dark colors require more maintenance because dirt and lint show up more easily. Twill and sturdy cottons can get lots of mileage in any hue for sofa upholstery, as can good-quality velvet, wool, and heavy felts. Consider a pattern in a bold color like red or deep maroon. Not only will it be attractive and make a statement, it will also prove less work than a light-colored fabric. Machine-washable slipcovers, rather than custom-upholstery, are another quality to look for in a sofa. They can be regularly washed for upkeep and are relatively inexpensive to change if you tire of a color or pattern. Leather, which gets softer and achieves a modulated, worn look with age, also works as a low-maintenance upholstery. Although once considered off-limits for its tendency to stain, new forms of machine-washable and stain-resistant ultrasuede can be used on sofas, too.

Make sure you like what you're buying as you'll use your sofa everyday. Never buy a piece furniture that you're unsure about. It is possible to find a sofa that is low-maintenance and comfortable, and will look polished and clean.

SOFA-SHOPPING CHECKLIST

- Bring a measuring tape! Make sure the sofa fits in the required space and through doorways.
- Pick a fabric that can stand wear and tear.
- Test drive before you buy! Sit down, stretch out, and relax before making a decision. Remember: You'll be spending lots of time here.
- Color is the easiest way to make a design statement in a room, whether it be a neutral tone; a bright, bold color; or a graphic pattern that can capture a child's imagination.
- Make sure the sofa fits the location. Proportions are key: Small-scale furniture in a small room can make it look even smaller. Conversely, oversized pieces in a large room don't necessarily fill up the space.
- Add a variety of textures to the sofa, with accessories such as soft wool or mohair throws, or pillows dressed up in cashmere. Small touches like these help make a room cozy and family-friendly.

the family room

From the most grandiose to the humblest of family rooms, comfort and versatility are key. A family room is a place where families can work, play, nap, and even dine now and then. It's a room where the family can convene and relax over any number of activities at once.

Although books and games are important to a modern family's leisure time, the TV is indisputably the primary form of entertainment for most families these days. If you prefer to limit TV watching, you can keep the set out of sight in a cabinet or in one of the many attractive armoires designed specifically for entertainment equipment. But if you accept that the TV plays an important role in your family's life, there's no need to hide it. Simply integrate it into your stylish decor. After all, TVs aren't as ugly as they used to be. And attractive, wall-mounted options like plasma-screen TVs are now available. Although expensive, these TVs free up floor space and eliminate clunky cords and wires so your children can play safely nearby. But if a plasma set isn't in your budget, try placing the television on a stand or table with stylish touches surrounding it. Pictures, flowers, or beautiful artifacts from your travels can be just as enticing here as anywhere else in the family room.

Designs That Convey Fun

In most homes, the family room is where low maintenance meets style, and so many different elements go into creating it, from books and games, to televisions and stereos, to key pieces of furniture, such as sofas, tables, and bookcases. It's an area that should have open spaces and invite relaxation. A pool table, like the one shown in the family room at the right, sets the tone for an informal space where games are meant to be played and fun is meant to be had. A pool table is a great draw for teenagers in particular, but if billiards isn't your style, you can just as easily have a table-tennis or air-hockey table—whatever suits you. A seat at the base of the stone fireplace adds relaxed seating to a room that would be equally comfortable hosting children or adults at play. (Notice the curved corners of the stone hearth that help reduce the danger of bumps and bruises when small children are around.) The tomes lining the bookcase also suggest that a family room can support quiet time as well. The room should be furnished with comfortable sofas, resilient fabrics, and smaller tables. Or, you can go without furniture to create a large, open space for play. Whether your children enjoy puzzles, blocks, or cars and racetracks, the floor is the space of choice for any number of such activities, especially when the children are small.

Open space and simple settings are equally viable as a room that's chockfull of electronic and gaming equipment. In a well-designed family room seen on page 52, there's room to pursue both daydreams and prime-time dreams, providing fertile ground for young imaginations. The throws on the sofa suggest that this room is for relaxing—and that napping is encouraged.

ABOVE A stone hearth and book-lined, wooden shelves create
a multitude of textures and a cozy atmosphere in this family
room. Comfortable upholstery in light, airy fabrics softens a
game room entrenched in stone like this one. But don't forget
room for play. Leave space for items like this pool table.

Vacation Home Family Rooms

Vacation homes, like any other type of home, also need casual, multipurpose family rooms. A rainy day when you're on vacation is twice as bad if children don't have enough room to play. Leave room in cabinets for storing games and puzzles. Furniture can be covered in lightweight cottons, and printed fabrics can be placed around the room, adding cheerful jolts of color. Director's chairs add inexpensive extra seating, while adding a nautical motif.

ABOVE The clearing in this family room, framed by the bucolic view through a large picture window, leaves a space worthy of imagination and allows ample room for play. Place simple chairs at either corner for extra seating that can easily be cleared for more room. A multicolored rug pulls this room together and helpfully disguises lint and dust.

OPPOSITE Classic nautical stripes set the casual tone in this family room. The white-painted rafters add informality to the dramatic ceilings and views, and the low, fabric-covered coffee table is big enough to accommodate games and puzzles. Kids will love to explore the seashells placed on the window ledge. Touches like these bring a bit of the outdoors in.

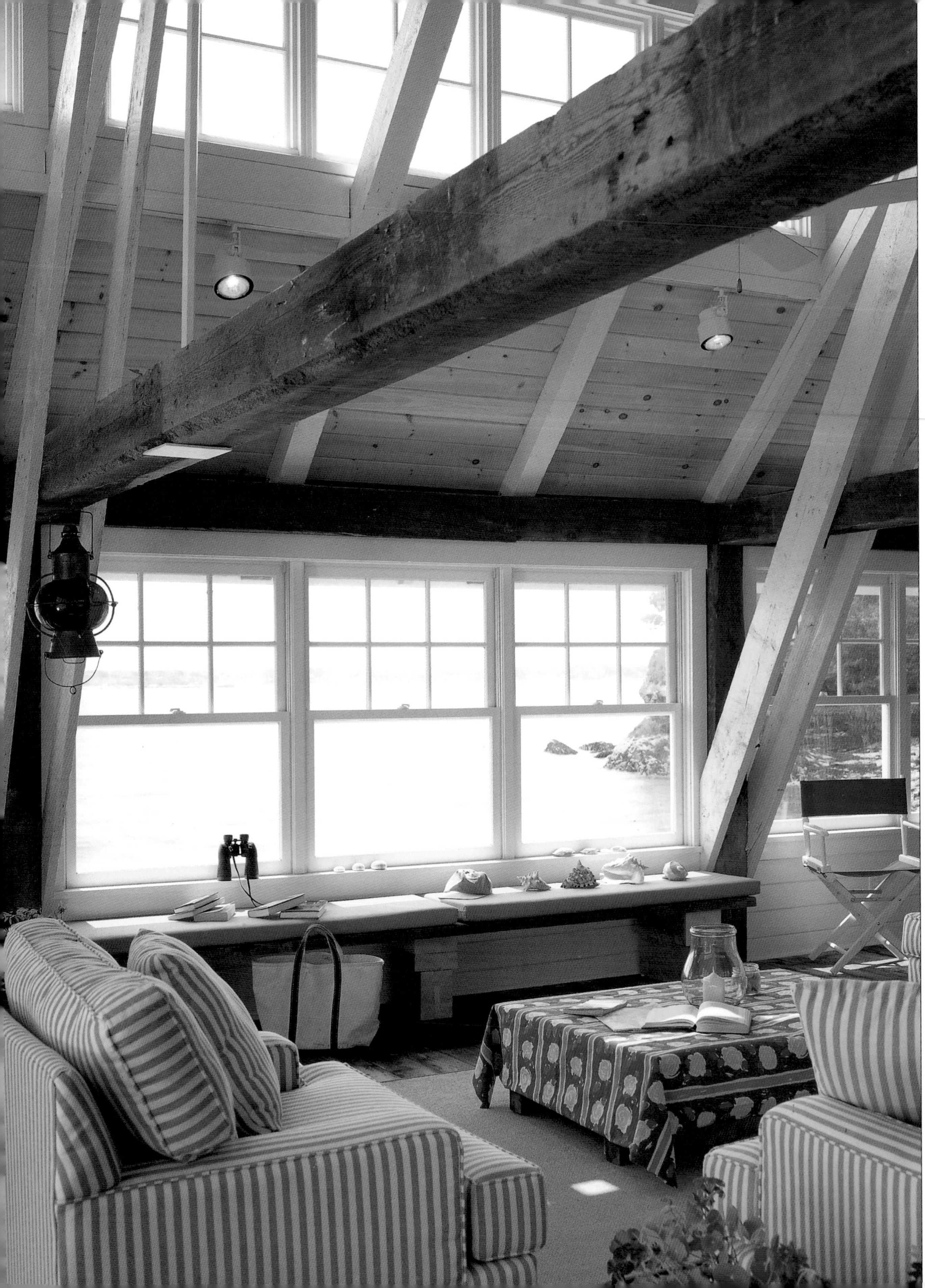

KID-FRIENDLY: fabrics

To accommodate the traffic of the living room, sturdy fabrics are needed. For the best results, upholstery should be a durable, heavy weave, easy to clean, and no-fuss. Other fabrics that work include twill, heavy-woven cotton, wool, felt, and leather in darker colors that have been stain-proofed. Patterns need less upkeep than solids, but the rest of the fabrics in the living room should follow suit. From window treatments to carpets to pillows, all of the living room's touches can be durable and still look sophisticated.

WINDOW TREATMENTS

Although not directly involved in most of the living room's action, the window treatments should still be considered fair game. You'll be surprised how they, too, can become targets for stains or spills. Blinds are an option to consider. Whether wood or aluminum, most require just an easy dusting to keep clean and are simple enough for any of your children to operate. They're resilient, too. Most blinds last a lifetime. But always be careful not to leave the cords hanging when small children might be in the room alone. Although more difficult to manage, curtains can still be had in the living room. Billowing silk curtains that hang to the floor or delicate and filmy gauze can be beautiful, but these may require more frequent cleaning. Consider heavy-duty cotton or darker colors. A shorter curtain that hangs to just the window instead of to the floor can be easier to deal with as well. Although less dramatic, they're easier to keep clean and less tempting to young fingers (or to hide-and-seek players). Remember: You want your living room to be played in and enjoyed, and not full of hands-off areas for your children.

FLOORING

Flooring also requires lots of consideration. If you're lucky enough to have hardwood floors in your home, you are a step ahead in the style department. They're not only beautiful but also easy to maintain. Just make sure you protect them by keeping them clean and putting felt protectors on the legs of chairs. An area rug will beautify any type of flooring, with low-pile or natural rugs being the easiest to maintain. Sisal, sea grass, or jute rugs come in natural tones that complement almost any room, and are available in dyed versions if you want a dose of color. Short-pile or flat, woven-wool rugs are also easy to maintain and come in a wide range of colors and patterns. For an ethnic vibe, flat-woven dhurries release dirt easily and are as easy to maintain as any natural floor covering. But if your heart is set on an Oriental rug, don't despair. Although you may want to put away the antique one until the kids are out of toddlerhood, a less-precious Oriental carpet can be quite durable. Simply stick with one-hundred percent wool, and give it a stain-resistant treatment.

OPPOSITE In this living room, dark wood and velvet uphol-stery project a sophisticated look against a canvas of neutral walls. Try placing a traditional rug in the center to create a cozy atmosphere.

ACCESSORIES

In the rest of the living room, pay attention to the accents, too. Pillows and throws should be pretty, but not necessarily precious. Delicate silk or light-colored fabrics are best reserved for a room that isn't used as often. But if you've been holding out on color for big items like sofas and walls, you can add that splash of intense color with your pillows or other decorations.

If you keep to fabrics sturdy enough for the rigors of family life, you'll have ample room for plenty of style so that your children can play undisturbed and your entire family can be comfortable for years to come in a stylish and easy-to-maintain living space.

KID-FRIENDLY FABRICS

- Machine-washable fabrics are always the best choice for slipcovers, curtains, and throw rugs.
- Cotton, twill, felt, and wool upholstery fabrics are easy to keep clean and can last a lifetime.
- If using leather, soften the look with velvet or cashmere pillows or a soft throw.
- Curtain fabric should be considered, too! Like upholstery, make sure it's resilient and easy to clean.
- Floor treatments in highly trafficked areas can be stylish and easily maintained. Try sisal, sea grass, or low-pile wool.
- Antique rugs and other precious heirloom fabrics aren't off-limits. Just make sure they're treated for stain resistance.
- Don't forget comfort! Soft throws and cozy pillows lend an inviting touch and are more comfortable for children to lounge on when reading or watching TV.
- Plants and greenery inject life into a room and help make the air healthier for the family to breathe.

the multipurpose room

Living rooms so often serve several purposes: a family room, a room in which to entertain, and a playroom. Paradoxically, for a family short on space, accommodating all the family's needs is easier if the room itself is simple. More functions don't have to mean more furniture. Versatility is key when it comes to combining needs in a single room. But how do you combine a living room, playroom, and even possibly an office into one space without the clutter?

Incorporating a Home Office

A corner of a room can easily be converted into an office space large enough for a desk, and still leave room for the usual living room pieces and allow activity to flow unimpeded. If you house the computer in an armoire, it can easily be concealed when you entertain guests. Whether you have a stand-alone desk or a storage unit, if you want your office furniture to be unobtrusive, choose it from a palette similar to the rest of the room. If the room is a white-on-white space, a neutral or white-toned desk would blend in best. Similarly, antique mahogany pieces are perfect for a darker color scheme. The more difficult task is preserving enough play area for children. Ideally, large, open spaces are best, but with sofas, desks, and other furniture already populating the room, the space can be crowded. Eliminating the coffee table and using only side tables next to the sofa can create larger, open areas for play. Cabinets, bookshelves, or roomy armoires will add plenty of shelving for storing and organizing toys and other games kept

in the living room. Armoires or chests with drawers are a great option for a modified toy bin, and still provide shelves for video games, books, DVDs, and the like.

Stackable bookshelves are also extremely useful. If necessary, another set of shelves can be added for more room, or they can be dismantled easily and moved elsewhere. Office furniture stores as well as home furnishings shops offer inexpensive bookcases that work by themselves or combine with several others to create a shelving system. If you use your living room for entertaining, try to find units with doors or drawers that shut so you can keep toys out of sight during adult time.

Maximizing Space

If you don't want to give up the coffee table to maximize floor space, use minimal furniture with a softened palette to allow movement and comfort. Leather club chairs piled with soft throws and cushions are as comfortable as an overstuffed sofa. Baskets underneath the coffee table can serve as storage for toys and games. Use an ottoman as a coffee table to eliminate hazardous sharp corners; it can fill in as extra seating if a crowd shows up. A low-maintenance carpet provides a padded area for a play space. Different textures, a variety of tones, and integrated furniture all come together to make a living room work to fulfill various needs.

ORGANIZING: storage solutions

Living rooms are meant for living. Living requires stuff, but not as much stuff as we usually manage to accumulate, so storage becomes a necessity in most family rooms. Try to plan for it. Items that tend to amass in the high-traffic living room include toys, books, videos, and magazines. Many other objects also find a temporary home here. But with a few additions of storage space, your living room can remain relatively clutter free.

In many homes, the living room is the media and entertainment center of the household, and that means CDs, DVDs, and video games inevitably end up there. Bookcases and racks made expressly for storing CDs can do the trick, but if you have small children, try to find closable racks or units that can be placed out of their reach. Toddlers love to empty shelves. Bookcases can hold family photos and other decorative accents, as well as books and media equipment. If you need additional space, stacked Lucite cubes or wall shelves near the stereo can help organize your collection without adding clutter. Small, stacking bookcases are ideal for smaller spaces, too. As objects accumulate, you can add another shelf or unit, building upward to save valuable floor space. Make sure tall furniture is stable, though. If not built in, it's best to bolt tall bookcases and bureaus to the wall. For televisions, it may be best to invest in an armoire or a media unit, complete with its own shelves and drawers to house the necessary accessories. Although many armoires are specifically designed to store entertainment systems, others can be modified to allow for electronics.

OPPOSITE A boldly patterned rug is the centerpiece in this airy living room. Narrow shelves are tucked in at the corners, alongside window seats, adding storage space and unobtrusive seating spaces.

STORAGE TIPS

· Try to combine function with form: a table that doubles as a storage trunk or a window seat that also encloses storage space can work wonders.

· Hang single shelves on a wall to display decorative objects without compromising floor space.

· Use colorful boxes and baskets to give the room style while doubling as storage space for magazines and other odds and ends.

· Be creative in finding storage solutions: under a coffee table, in an armoire, perhaps even in baskets under the couch.

· Bookshelves and étagères are great ways to display books and objects. Use the higher shelves to hold valuable items and the lower shelves to hold the children's books and toys.

· An armoire or console can be a versatile piece of furniture. Make sure when purchasing one that it can fulfill all your needs.

· Seating is important to a room. Try to add comfortable places to sit by adding cushions to a window seat or piling large floor pillows in a corner.

A smaller bookshelf, a corner étagère, or a wall shelf in a bright color or an unusual design can create an interest point as well as add storage space. It's also nice to keep extra throw pillows, coverlets, board games, and puzzles at hand. Before overstuffing the existing bookcases, consider some other options. Storage trunks can easily double as side or coffee tables, housing board games that are rarely used, extra pillows or blankets that help transition a room from spring to winter, and other rarely used items. They'll be out of sight, but still accessible, if needed. Two-tiered tables are another possibility. Add baskets below for greater organization. A few magazines, books, or even toys can be stashed in them, providing easy access. Attractive, stacked boxes or baskets can serve the same purpose.

Magazine racks or baskets can also give a stylish or daring touch to a living room. Wall-mounted or standing racks take up little room, but they can provide lots of storage space. For a rustic touch and an easy place to stow toys during cleanup, consider scattering baskets around the living area. A quick sweep is all it takes to tidy up for evening guests.

4 UTILITARIAN spaces

It's easy to overlook the spaces where the necessary minutiae of life take place: the entrance to the house, the place you hang your coat or place your keys, the hallway that stores hats and gloves, or the bathroom where you start your day each morning. Despite their small size, many of these spaces do affect your life. The mudroom, laundry space, bathroom, and other nooks and crannies that you don't often think about in the grand scheme of decorating are often areas where you spend lots of time without even realizing it. Think about the time it takes to get ready to go in the morning and ready for bed in the evening: If forty-five minutes daily doesn't seem like much, add it up. It's almost eight hours a week, thirty-two hours a month, and four-hundred hours a year! That's more than two weeks! And the mudroom is where the entire family enters and leaves the house every day. You may not spend long periods of time there, but as the last place you see before leaving your home and the first place you see upon returning, it assumes greater significance—and even ten minutes a day adds up quickly.

But before you drive yourself crazy with mathematical equations, think instead about how every little space in your home matters for you and for your kids. Even the most seemingly mundane space serves a utilitarian purpose. After all, a home should be enjoyed in every respect, and that means looking after all its respective parts.

The key to maximizing such spaces lies in the organization of each individual space. A highly efficient laundry room not only makes cleaning simpler, it may even make the chore of doing laundry more enjoyable. A mudroom that's a disorganized pile of mittens and soccer cleats can become an ordered storage haven, and a well-organized bathroom can only make your daily time there more pleasant, even for the kids. With organization, these spaces also become more user-friendly for them, too, especially places like mudrooms and hallways that they use often.

OPPOSITE Place a simple, wooden bench at the entrance of the house to serve as storage for rain gear and other assorted belongings. Paint the floor an interesting color, like this cheery yellow, to contrast with the gloom of rainy days.

function
meets style

But what truly transforms these spaces is a decorative makeover. A splash of color, wallpaper, or other painted details you don't want to indulge in the main rooms of the house can have full reign here. Because these spaces are out of sight from most guests, you have the chance to be a bit daring. Think of it as an experimental part of decorating the house. If an idea you're hesitant to use on a larger scale makes you too nervous to try elsewhere, give it a chance here. Funky shelving, feminine floral details, or bold chrome fixtures are all viable possibilities. And the utilitarian rooms of the house, no longer ignored or forgotten, will soon rival the rest of the house in their style and comfort for the whole family.

Giving order to a space while adding a touch of whimsy not only streamlines the way your family lives but also puts a smile on your face or bestows a few minutes of serenity as you enter or leave your house or as you do a daily chore. And you should never underestimate the importance of that.

LEFT Transform an entrance into a sometime mudroom. Even just a small closet, a rustic umbrella stand, and a wooden footstool can make the entryway useful as a mudroom. Lay down a doormat to keep from trekking in debris from the outside world.

mudroom

The classic mudroom probably proliferated first in New England. Northeasterners like their grand entrances as well as anyone else, but with the frequency of murky weather and with a mud season to contend with, a more casual side entrance as a place to store dirty footwear and winter layers must have emerged as an alternative to sullying the pristine main entrance and foyer. The rest of us caught on quickly, amending our side entrances even without the temperamental springs and winters of the Northeast.

But the first mudrooms of yore have quickly grown up into catchalls that both complete and organize a modern household. In the largest examples, the addition of hooks, tables, mail slots, and message centers have transformed mudrooms into sophisticated anterooms. And if your house doesn't come with one, be creative. If you can fit in a few hooks and attractive baskets or cubbies into the entrance hall, that space can easily transform into a transitional space where pet supplies, backpacks, schoolbooks, sporting equipment, and shoes can be accommodated.

Storage

Closets, closets, and more closets are the most helpful way to arrange a mudroom. Seasonal items that most likely won't be used as often—like ski equipment and tennis rackets—can be stored away on shelves, in boxes, or in other crannies. A row of pegs or hooks can help arrange coats or umbrellas. A small table for keys, mail, and other objects should be placed near the entrance. A shoe rack, umbrella stand, or hamper also helps matters during the wetter months.

Entrance Hall

Even if you don't have the luxury of a mudroom, entrance halls are still transitional spaces, and they can be encouraged to function as such. A closet or shelving will help streamline the daily detritus. Inexpensive, easy-to-clean flooring is a must. Opt for attractive doormats, washable area rugs, or a painted and sealed floor cloth. Or if possible, redo the flooring with water-sealed ceramic tiles; cleaning will never be easier. Shaker-style pegs or hooks are helpful too—especially if closet space is lacking. Cubbies or baskets for shoes help reduce the flow of dirt into the rest of the house.

RIGHT Add shelves, cubbyholes, and sliding wire baskets to help arrange belongings in the mudroom. Use the closet space to hang coats, and add a low bench to help the transition from muddy boots to clean house slippers.

ORGANIZING: family message center

If the key to easy, efficient living is staying organized, then there is nothing better than having a space in the home dedicated to just that in a message center. It's a miniature news kiosk where soccer games, business dinners, and PTA meetings get recorded so that everyone in the family is aware of family happenings, making communication simple so that nothing falls between the cracks.

LOCATION

An entry foyer or a corner of the kitchen may seem like the most logical place for a message center, but really it should be wherever makes sense for your family. Underneath a second-floor landing, in the living room, or on the wall of an office are all possibilities. Anywhere you can fit a board for posting messages and invitations or a calendar will work. Do put it in a central location, though, so that everyone in the family sees it regularly without having to make a special trip for it. With a little improvisation, you can make it an asset to your home rather than an eyesore. A French-style upholstered board that is quilted with ribbons offers an attractive way to integrate a message center into a room's decor. Daintily pretty, crisscrossed ribbons allow invitations, photos, and papers to be posted in its corners. A corkboard can be covered in any fabric of your choosing and surrounded with a painted wood frame. A magnetized surface such as the refrigerator works just as easily, though. Add an oversize calendar to keep a visible reminder of family appointments, and invest in some fun magnets.

HIGH-TECH COMMUNICATION

A corner of the office or den is also a spot where family messages and calendars can keep everyone up to speed. If spreadsheets and computer printouts are your primary mode of communication, the message board should be located where it is convenient to the computer. Just make sure that a board or a part of the wall surface is kept clear for posting messages in the open for everyone to see. And even if the message board is located in what is primarily a work space, family photos and artwork can still figure into the mix to keep things cheerful.

OPPOSITE Liven up a message board with bits of ribbon and colorful pictures. Bookshelves and boxes in this family work space store both office supplies and kids' art supplies. Spice up a message board with a fun design like this diamond-pattern board.

laundry room

In households with children, the stream of laundry to be done is never ending. But there's no reason why a working laundry room shouldn't be cheerful, too. First, for functionality, the laundry room should have several shelves and durable, waterproof surfaces. If you have a laundry-size sink at your disposal, a waterproof working space nearby for laying items flat before they're hung can come in handy. A place to stow baskets or a built-in laundry hamper minimizes the need to carry heavy loads of clothing, too. Add a stool or chair to the mix to allow a little break for daydreaming or for some company, especially for the children. Bright lights, a folding table, and a fold-out ironing board (which can also conserve valuable space) are other essentials. As in the kitchen, remember to keep detergent, bleach, and other potentially hazardous substances out of the reach of children. A high shelf or even a cabinet with a safety lock will suffice.

Decorative Touches

Touches like pretty framed prints, plants, and striped or brightly painted walls add cheer to your work space. Go from drab to daring with funky striped walls or interesting prints. If there's a space between the cabinets and the ceiling, don't neglect it! Potted plants or bright borders complete the overall effect. A framed print that doesn't fit in elsewhere in the house could be perfect here. A message board with reminders, lists, and pictures is a good way to prompt some thinking while you fold laundry. Add touches of whimsy by hanging vintage or antique laundry artifacts or signs. Flea markets, antique fairs, or yard sales are great places to scavenge for these. Even the tiniest odds and ends of rustic Americana can give your laundry room a lively, countrified look that is more appealing than white, sanitary, and dull. Vintage plaques, pieces of patchwork quilt, or wicker can also add interest to a laundry room, as can delicately feminine drawings and Victorian-style baskets hung on the walls.

LEFT Add interesting details to give an otherwise pure-white laundry room a bit of pizzazz. The hamper doors that resemble whitewashed shutters, bright prints, and an antique washing board propped against the wall enliven this room. Baskets and glass jars hold loose ends, whereas a simple bulletin board is perhaps the best accessory, holding family pictures and mementos.

OPPOSITE Down to the drain in the middle of the floor, this workroom is highly functional and completely waterproof, but the jazzy waves and portholes of the paint job keep it far from dreary utilitarianism.

kids' bathrooms

Like the laundry room, the bathroom shouldn't be thought of as purely functional. It's as important for kids to feel comfortable and at home here as in any other part of the house. Make the bathroom a pleasurable, comfortable place to be, and before you know it, your children will forget that washing up used to be a chore. Just as it's important for you to have relaxing downtime in the bath, it's equally important for kids!

Proportion and Size Considerations

The most common problem in kids' bathrooms is negotiating the proportions. Adult-size sinks, countertops, and cabinets are gigantic for a 4-year-old, just as something built for a 4-year-old is outgrown by the time the child turns 8 or 9. Try to find ways to make the bathroom accessible for everyone. This usually means adding a step stool, but it could also mean installing adjustable touches like hooks, towel racks, and handles at child-friendly heights, which can always be moved up later. Or, if you have room, a free-standing towel rack might be easier to add.

OPPOSITE Turn small corners into storage space with narrow cabinets like these, but make sure to put medicine on high shelves. Plastic hampers and lots of hooks help to further organize the space.

KID-FRIENDLY: waterproof surfaces

Messiness in a child's bathroom, a laundry room, or a mudroom is understandably a given. But making sure surfaces in those rooms are waterproof and safe is a must. Test out the surfaces of floors, bathtubs, and showers before children have a go in them. If the surfaces are slippery, add a rubber-backed or skid-resistant mat to catch little feet before they have a chance to skid.

Ceramic tiling on the floor, walls, and counters of a bathroom, mudroom, or laundry room is easy to clean, available in endless color options, and waterproof as long as the tiles are properly sealed. On floors, however, they may be slippery, so remember to add bath mats or nonskid, canvas coverings to ensure safety.

Although marble is a pricier option, it's also easy to maintain. Its slick, grainy appearance can lend a more serious air to a bathroom. Even in tiny doses—for example, on countertops or in the shower—marble gives a bathroom or any other space a timeless appeal.

In bathrooms, treated wood is an option for cabinetry, walls, and even counters, but it's probably best to reserve wooden floors for other parts of the house. Laminated plywood can be made over in lots of colors and is as water resistant as a tiled or marble surface for countertops. Wooden floors in a mudroom are acceptable and have a rustic appeal as long as they've been treated and floor coverings or entrance mats are in place so that feet can be wiped clean before entering.

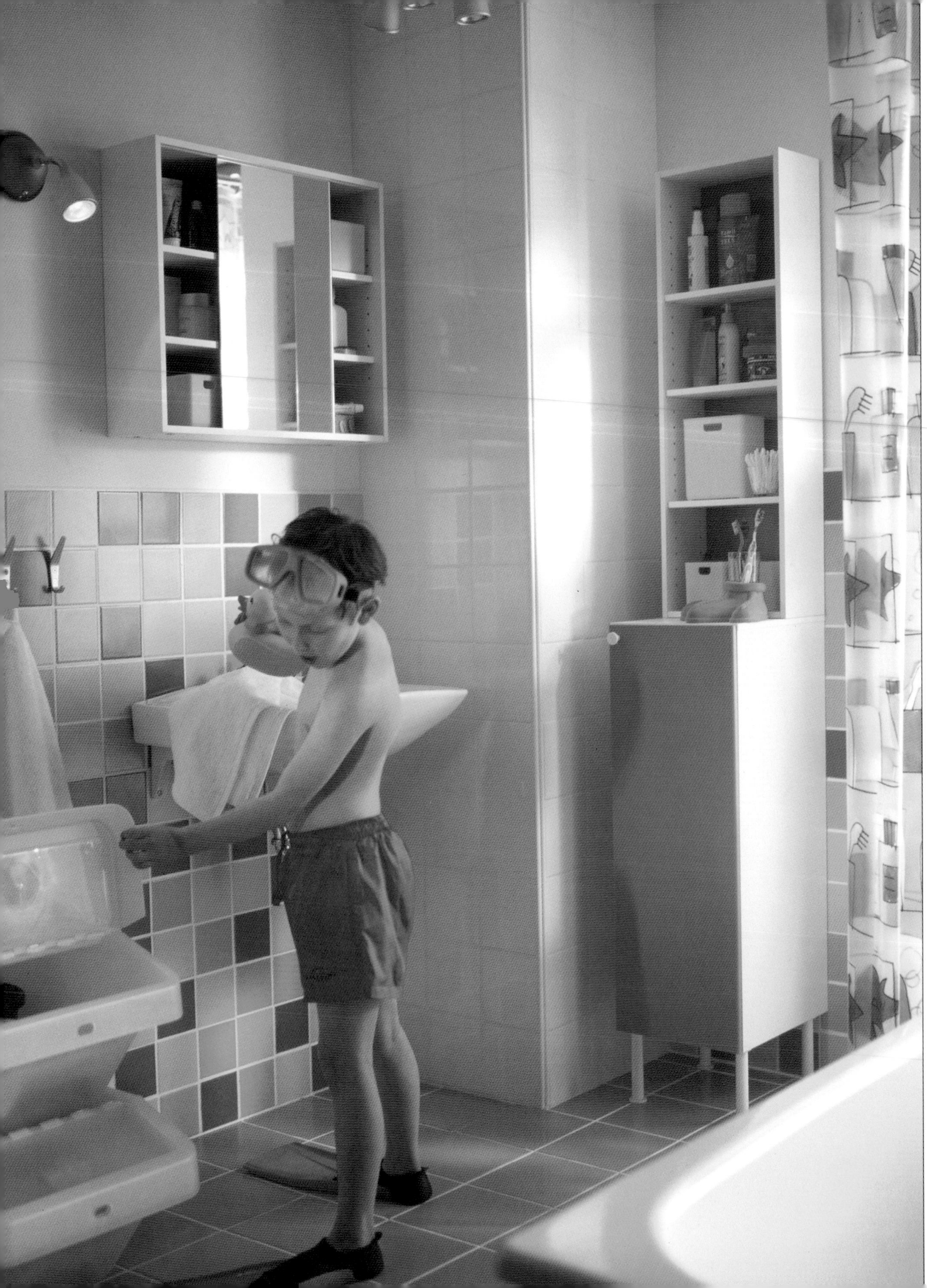

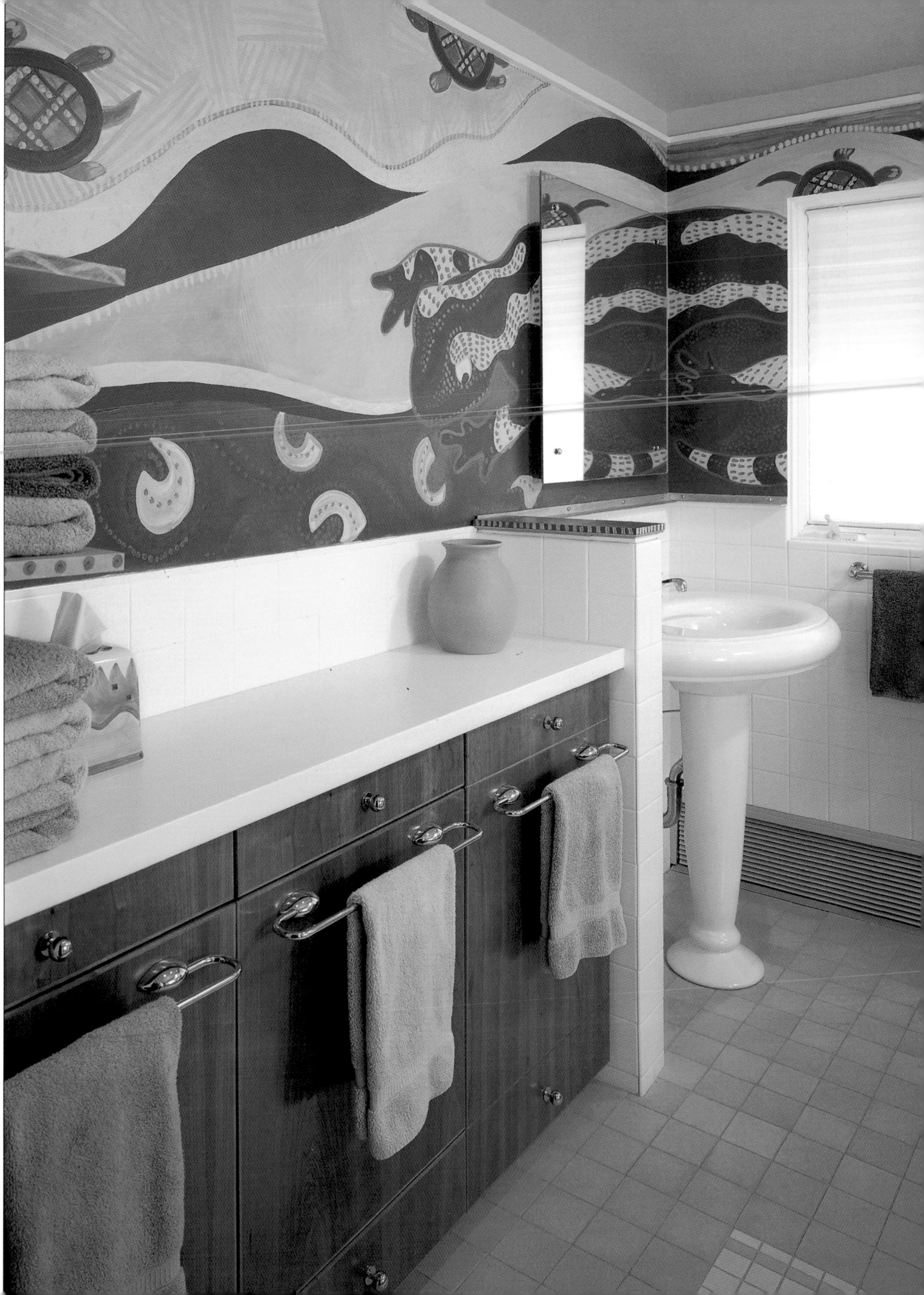

Kids' Creativity for the Bedroom

Because kids' bathrooms are less visible than other rooms in the house, their decor can get creative and even a little funky. Be sure your children know that their opinions are always welcome, but make this especially so in rooms meant primarily for their use. Bright colors, painted designs, and colorful toys can be included in the bathroom area. Shower curtains and bath rugs are easy ways to brighten the space. You can even let your kids personalize their area by painting it themselves. A wall of colored handprints from their younger years could remain as nostalgic handmade wallpaper for years to come.

Organized Storage for a Small Space

As you create a welcoming space, storage and a functional layout are also important considerations in the bathroom. Because fun often goes hand-in-hand with messiness, a well-organized bathroom that's kid-friendly is a challenge to maintain, but it doesn't have to be impossible. Make sure you provide lots of shelves, cabinets, or baskets for organization. Hampers for dirty clothes and towels are a must. If your bathroom is short on space, try baskets underneath the sink or hung on the back of a door. For young children, having toys and waterproof books close at hand in the bath is key to making the bath an enjoyable experience. Install a storage space to hold all the bath accessories. A short plastic cart with pullout drawers does the trick if it can be placed next to the tub.

OPPOSITE Let your imagination go with a bright-and-bold mural. The outsize salamanders and turtles announce that this is a child's space, but they're sophisticated enough to appeal to adults, too. And with plenty of shelves for storing towels and other bathroom essentials, practicality isn't overlooked.

RIGHT Hang a woven laundry basket on the back of a bathroom door that needs to conserve valuable floor space. Wet towels and clothing will be ready for washing without cluttering the floor.

SHOPPING: fixtures and fittings

A bathroom's fixtures and fittings are important in creating the look that you want. From stainless steel to brass to nickel, everything from the bathroom's faucet to the towel racks will gleam with the metal finish you choose. Regardless of the material, however, it's probably best to keep a uniform look for all fittings. This will bring any other disparate materials together and help the bathroom look cohesive. For example, wooden cabinets, bright blue tiles, and a frosted glass shower may seem like an over-the-top combination, but with the same metal-toned fittings bringing it all together, the bathroom looks like a made-to-order dream.

METAL COLOR CHOICES

Depending on what look you want to achieve, silver- or gold-colored fixtures and fittings will make a difference. Brass and copper tones can give a warmer feeling to a bathroom, whereas stainless steel and nickel can project cool sophistication. If you can't decide between them, two-tone fittings will make the grade. Different metals range greatly in price, however, so beware. Stainless steel is generally much less expensive than similar-looking nickel, and gold-plated metals are lower on the price spectrum than brass or copper. But if you decide to keep costs on the low side, there's no need to sacrifice looks. Shop around. Many stores today offer complete lines of affordable fittings and fixtures in a variety of traditional and modern looks. If there's room in your budget for pricier options, look at top-of-the-line manufacturers such as Waterworks, Dornbracht, or British import Czech and Speake. Any of these are sure to meet your style needs and should be durable enough to serve the whole family for years.

STYLE AND CONSISTENCY

What style of fixture should you choose? A funkier, more modern look may be a fun choice in the children's bathroom, but a more traditional style would carry the bathroom through years of different paint jobs and adjusting tastes. As when picking finish colors, the best choice is to remain consistent throughout the bathroom. A futuristic-looking faucet may look strange with Federal-style molding or wainscoted walls. Similarly, super-slick fittings in a rustic, wood-outfitted bathroom would also seem out of place.

When winding down the home stretch of decorating the bathroom, or any room for that matter, it may seem like the best choice is the easiest, but consider the wealth of options out there before making a final decision. Just remember: In a small space like a bathroom, pulling together a stylish, kid-friendly space is all in the details.

OPPOSITE Place freshly washed towels at the ready for guests, and add touches like fresh flowers or sweet-smelling soaps to make anyone who uses the room—guest or family—feel at peace.

shared bathrooms

Things undoubtedly get a little more complicated when there is more than one person using a bathroom. In an ideal world, there would be a bathroom for each person in the house, but the reality is that sharing is unavoidable in most households. Sharing space in the bathroom can be difficult if you have an inquisitive 5-year-old and a cosmetic-happy teenager sharing storage space, or if you have a mix of teenage boys and girls who all want their privacy. The best solution is to design the bathroom to be versatile enough to suit many needs.

To begin, double sinks are a necessity. They'll double any bathroom's productivity by allowing for simultaneous teeth brushing and hair combing and can generally alleviate Monday-morning mayhem. If possible, each child should have his or her own set of drawers, storage space, and towel bar or hook to ensure that there's some sense of privacy. If there aren't enough drawers for that, try different-colored storage caddies stowed in a cabinet or on a shelf. A bathroom that connects between two children's rooms is a plus. Both have their own entrance and at least the illusion that the bathroom is their own.

LEFT Two of everything in this bathroom, down to the cubbyholes, lets kids divide space equally. By adding open storage space, you'll free up counter space, and still keep stored items visible. Let kids add their own touches, like the beanbag toys at the windowsill, to personalize their space.

OPPOSITE Pair chrome fittings with minimalist, sand-colored tiles and warm, brown paint for a sophisticated, contemporary look. This extra-large sink works well in a shared bathroom.

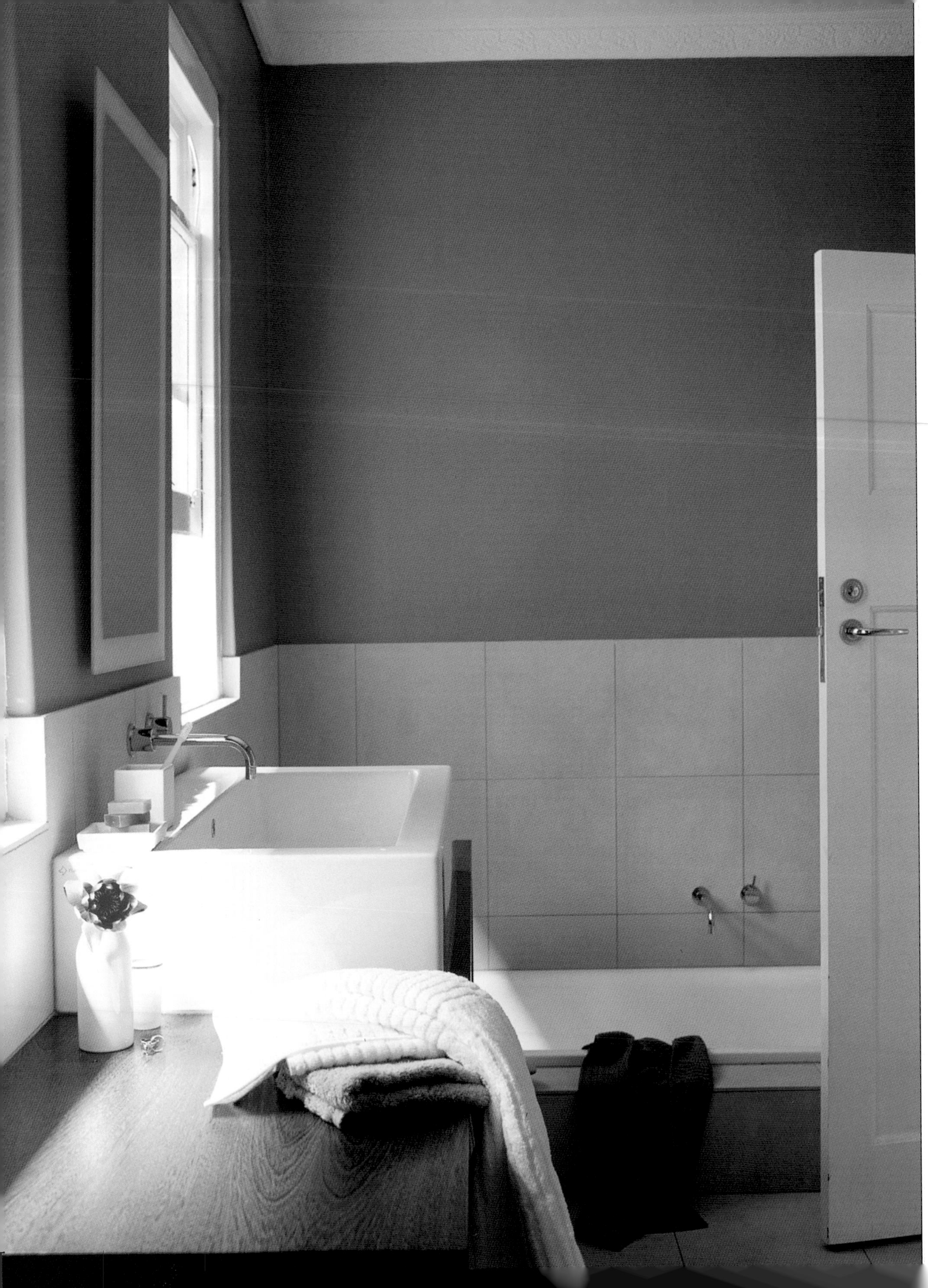

A Parents', Kids', and Guest Bathroom

If adults and children will be sharing a bathroom, it's important to make it comfortable for people of all ages. Toys can be kept to a minimum, along with any other bathroom clutter. Swap stuffed animals for framed prints for a more sophisticated look. Make sure the bathroom is as soothing and welcoming to children as it is to adults.

If a bathroom will double as a guest bathroom, make it especially user-friendly. Clean towels should be readily available as well as soaps and shampoos. Storage space remains important, but glass cabinets can be a more inviting choice, because they allow guests to feel that they're welcome to use anything in the bathroom and they won't feel like they are snooping.

No matter what the look or the purpose of your bathroom, make sure it's a comfortable space. From colorful and playful to white and serene, a bathroom should be as functional as it is attractive.

ABOVE One brilliant way to deal with multiple users is to create a separate room within the bathroom for the shower or bath. This shower room makes it possible for one person to shower while another uses the outer bathroom area. The cobalt blue wall helps define the shower as a separate space, enhancing a sense of privacy.

OPPOSITE If you pare down to your top priorities, storage can always be found for what is essential. This bedroom has largely been pared down to two essentials: storing an extensive record collection and providing a serene sleeping space. An old army chest adds a graphic touch and a bit of extra storage at the foot of the bed.

STYLE FILE: storage solutions

In any utilitarian space, storage is paramount, and finding attractive and colorful ways to store things is a prized ability. Drawers, boxes, and cubbyholes are musts, everywhere from the sparest of mudrooms to the most cluttered of bathrooms. In small rooms, maximizing the space you do have is essential. Stack boxes on shelves to store away extra papers and knickknacks. Cubbyholes or pullout shelves are another way to store items while keeping them easily accessible.

BOXES

Boxes are one way to store items that are used less frequently. Placed on shelves and in cabinets, they let you further organize your storage spaces and keep visual clutter to a minimum. In the bathroom, they can hold necessary but little-used medicines and first-aid equipment. In a laundry room, sewing equipment that should be kept out of reach of children finds the perfect home in a series of stacked boxes. If you want your children to have access to what has been stored in the boxes, put labels (or pictures) that they can read on the boxes. And, whether you like them in wood, striped cardboard, or painted galvanized metal, storage boxes can add another colorful touch to your decor.

CUBBYHOLES

Cubbyholes are another innovative way to expand storage in a shelving unit. Where once only a stack of towels or a few hats would fit, cubbyholes inserted into a space can increase storage tenfold. A mudroom benefits from superefficient cubbyholes that separate hats from gloves from scarves, so they're easy to find when you're rushing out the door. Likewise, in a bathroom, clean towels are ready to grab as soon as you step out of the shower.

THE IMPORTANCE OF BEING EFFICIENT

The tiny work spaces of a home are just as important to the entire family's well-being as any other part of the house. From mudrooms to entrance halls to laundry rooms, a stylish space that serves its needs is the epitome of a well-run household. And don't forget to love those parts of the house like any other. They're the cogs that make the rest of the house function well, and they deserve to be treated as such. Paying attention to style and function in these utilitarian rooms is a surefire way to help your home become what it needs to be for your family to enjoy it to the fullest extent possible.

OPPOSITE Place a small set of cubbyholes atop a desk to help organize supplies—in this case for sewing. The soft green paint blends with the wall and is the perfect foil for the bright colors of the thread and ribbon.

5 QUIET time

At times, everyone needs a quiet refuge in which to get things done. Adults need space to do paperwork brought from the office, to pay bills, and to write letters. Children need space to do homework, often on a computer. With more and more people working from home and with the increasing dependence on computers, which must find a home somewhere, the home office has evolved into a necessity rather than a luxury. Creating a welcoming home without areas that are off-limits is important, but having a quiet and comfortable office or study to which you retreat for private time or a chance to organize matters of the home or career helps keep your home harmonious.

OPPOSITE A small desk in a corner may be all the home-office space you need. Place attractive containers on the desk and a useful bracket shelf above to maximize storage. The pale green walls are serene, whereas the bright-blue desk energizes the space.

your "quiet time" needs

A requirement of the office or study is that it enable concentration, especially for taking phone calls and other business activities if you work at home. An enclosed space is highly desirable. Even if the area is tiny, the essentials—a desk, a chair, a computer, bookshelves, and some file storage—can fit in a space the size of a small closet. But if you can't have a room all your own, try sectioning off a larger room with a partition or some other type of divider that gives you the feeling of privacy. Think, too, about the type of work you'll be doing. Are you a freelance writer who needs lots of room for manuscripts and brainstorming? Make the space or room bright and airy, and maybe add a large desk and several bookshelves. Or, do you run a business that requires constant communication? Get plenty of file cabinets and storage space for your documents, and reserve areas for your fax machine, computer, and other necessities. Or perhaps the office is primarily used for paying bills and organizing the household. Will a file drawer and cubby slots be helpful? Will your children be free to use the office for homework or computer games? Specially designated storage space for their things can reduce clutter. Whatever your situation, the home office should conform to your needs, and the more you plan in advance, the more likely you are to adequately meet those needs.

Consider the Work Environment

Think about what surroundings help you to concentrate, particularly when it comes to color. Pick a soothing hue for your work space. A sterile environment never fosters creativity. Channel the things that make you feel peaceful, and translate them into the room. Are you enamored of nature? Fill the room with plants, and hang botanical prints on the walls. Does the ocean have a tranquilizing effect? Paint the walls a frothy sea blue, and furnish it with seashells and other nautical accents. Use your creativity. If blocky furniture isn't your taste, substitute a comfortable upholstered chair. Use an armoire to store your computer so it can be locked out of sight if you don't like its look. But most important, make your home office feel like a little haven where time to yourself can be both productive and calming.

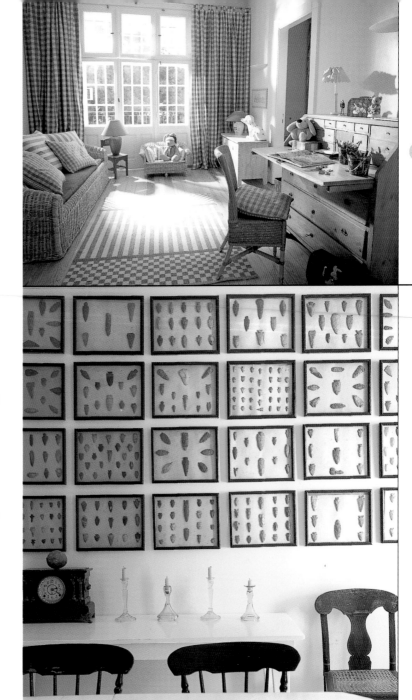

TOP Use the same fabric all over, like the gingham check that hangs at the windows, covers the cushions, and is stretched across the floor in this room. It unifies a room with more than one function. A desk with a pullout drawer and a daybed allow an easy transformation from work area to bedroom.

ABOVE Hang artwork or decorations symmetrically on the walls to make a statement. Here, antique arrowheads are placed on parchment-paper backgrounds to offer inspiration to those who work in this space. Pair neutral tones with a bright background, like this yellow, for a maximum effect.

OPPOSITE Bright accents against white walls create a soothing feel in an artist's studio. Artwork and decorative accents above the mantel keep it from being an eyesore. Stow paints in corner when not in use, and use a dining table for a work space.

SHOPPING: desks and bookcases

From corporate-style desk units to painted wooden bookshelves to stainless-steel grid shelving, there are millions of furniture choices to outfit your home office. Consider the size, comfort, and functional aspects before buying. Look for drawers and shelves on a desk, but also note its height to make sure you won't strain your back while working. Ample surface area that fits the necessary equipment, from the computer to the fax to a desktop lamp, is also necessary. Make sure that you don't feel cramped and that there's plenty of room for you to work.

DESK STYLES AND MATERIALS

Desk units built expressly to accommodate desktop computers are another option. Armoires with a pull-down work surface or even the simplest Parsons table can be outfitted with the necessary accoutrements to give a desk a custom-made vibe. Some even have pullout drawers for keyboards that can be attached to the desk, as well as other convenient details.

Materials for desk units also run the gamut. A classic, wooden secretary desk looks elegant and hides clutter easily, but it has less work space; stainless-steel surfaces accessorized with funky, bright colors can alter the look of a room completely. Furniture you already own or find at a secondhand store can be refurbished. Paint wood a different color to match the rest of the furniture, or refinish an antique desk in a dark shade for more sober tones. If you're buying a new desk, examine it for durability. Do drawers roll smoothly? Will they still operate well when they're full of heavy paper?

BOOKSHELVES

Bookshelves and storage units are other major pieces you'll want to dwell on. A study with lots of book space can make for a striking effect. Take stock of your floor space and the size of your book collection before buying. Note the dimensions of the shelves to ensure that they can hold all your books, and that you can double-load if necessary. If you have a lot of oversize books, look for adjustable shelves. Make sure bookcases don't overpower the room. If you're feeling hesitant about covering the room in books, try shorter shelves that can be stacked higher if needed. Lacking floor space? Then try bracket shelves or recessed bookcases that won't intrude on the rest of the room, or alternate a stack of books with details like potted plants and photographs. If you have small children, all tall bookshelves or storage units should be fastened to the wall so they won't topple.

OPPOSITE Make your desk a statement piece by painting it blueberry blue like this scallop-trim desk from Maine Cottage, a furniture company. Little details can give a piece of furniture a whole new attitude. Pair it with Maine Cottage's Boothbay chair in orange for more punch.

HINTS FOR THE HOME OFFICE

- Assess how much storage space you need, and buy accordingly.

- Bring a measuring tape—height, width, and depth are all important. And be sure to write down your measurements from home when you go shopping.

- Make sure the available surface area accommodates everything from computers to lamps to paperwork.

- Look for a pullout shelf for your computer keyboard to save on space.

- Use stackable bookcases for a growing library.

- Add bracket shelves to substitute for artwork in the library.

- Bring out the color—paint a wooden desk a sprightly shade, or stain it a rich, chocolate brown.

family home office

When you get down to the basics, work is still work, and it takes a conducive atmosphere to get it all done. A home office needs to be quiet and comfortable. Balance your work needs with details that make you feel at home, and allow the space to blend with the rest of the house's decor. Put a warm carpet under your desk, and add a throw to your office chair. You should always feel at ease. Artwork is always welcome, as are stylish storage units. Even computer manufacturers have gotten design savvy, from Apple's colorful Power Macs to wafer-thin laptops, proving that the home office can look good and still be a place to get the job done.

Comfortable furniture is a must. Test out different chairs to make sure they're good for your posture and won't strain your back or neck while you log long hours on the computer. Don't assume the furniture has to look corporate, either. It's your home. Furnish it as you like. An oversize antique leather chair is just as at home in the office as a modular desk. An adjustable office chair can be comfortable for users of every age and height. If you like the comfort of an office chair but can't bear the look, you could try rigging a slipcover. Don't forget to test out desk height. Straining to work at a low desk is just as uncomfortable as a blocky chair. Make sure comfort is a priority, and style will follow.

Get Organized

Getting organized is another priority. Streamline your office or study, and you'll accumulate less clutter. Look for desks with storage units attached if you have mountains of paperwork that needs to be organized. Rolling file cabinets are also useful and can be tucked underneath a simple table desk or stowed away in a closet when not in use. Bibliophiles must invest in bookcases. Paperwork in file boxes can also be stowed out of sight in cabinets. Bracket shelves hung on the wall also adds storage space for books. Add framed pictures and plants to beautify the entire room. Fabric-covered or painted boxes add a decorative touch and are a departure from boring office neutrals. If the room's walls already sport a standout color, all-white or black accents will complement it nicely.

LEFT Ergonomic office chairs like this one can translate from the boardroom to the home office easily, and your back will thank you. Combine office furniture with warm wooden cabinets, plants, and a stylish, marble-topped desk to avoid an excessively corporate look.

ORGANIZING: family documents

Important paperwork accumulates quickly—medical records, schoolwork, travel documents, and financial records—and it's a lot to organize. To keep tabs on your family, it's essential to get efficiently organized, especially as your children get older. Don't just throw it all together in an office drawer. If you do, you'll never find that immunization record when your child is ready to head off for camp next summer or that Little League application you've just realized is due tomorrow.

One way to get started is to keep binders or hanging files for every member of the family, as well as for different household matters. Finances should be kept separately from medical forms, and all should be clearly labeled. You may even want to color code binders to correspond to each member of the family. Then they, too, will know which set of documents pertains to them. Try to keep everything inside clearly labeled and in chronological order, as well as up-to-date. It only takes a few minutes to add the latest paperwork to its corresponding folder when it's processed. Otherwise, you may find yourself swamped with stacks of documents that eventually take a whole rainy afternoon to organize. You'll thank yourself later for organizing now. If there's room, reserve a shelf or a drawer for each member of the family, too.

If you'd like to keep some papers in a confidential spot, invest in a desk or armoire with a lock so that your important papers are out of sight when not in use. Perhaps a series of shuttered file cabinets will do the trick. A fireproof safe for the most important documents can be a good idea. It can be stowed deep in a closet, out of sight. How often do you need to look at the title to your house, anyway?

RX FOR FAMILY DOCUMENTS

- Separate paperwork into categories—for example, medical forms, financial records, and schoolwork.
- Use labeled binders for each family member.
- Make sure all paperwork is up-to-date and filed chronologically, to keep your documents efficiently organized.
- Don't wait for a rainy day to put paperwork in its place. File each document as it comes your way.
- File all documents concerning the entire family in a separate binder.
- Stow confidential papers safely out of sight in a locked armoire, desk, or file cabinet.
- Keep an oversize portfolio for each child's "artwork" to prevent it from piling up and to keep it safe.

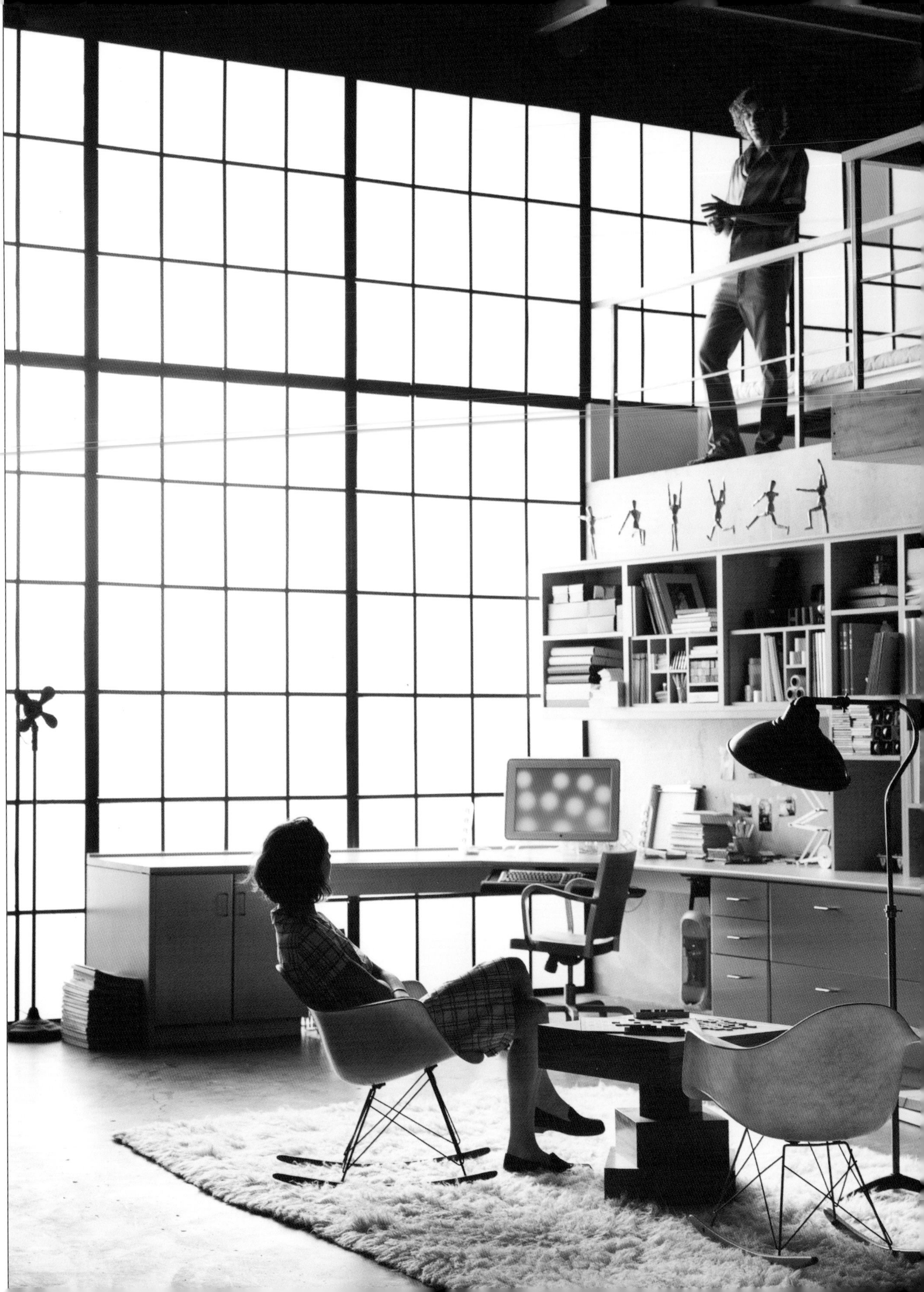

KID-FRIENDLY: lighting

You'll want to be sure your children's eyes aren't strained by excessive glare or lighting that's too dim. During the day, natural sunlight is best, but at night make sure the office, or any room, has plenty of bright light. Try to minimize or eliminate large variations and shady corners. Having to make rapid adjustments from light to dark areas can strain one's eyesight. Make sure the area surrounding the computer is bright, too, to avoid glare from the screen.

Overhead lights are harsh and should be eliminated or rarely used, particularly if there's a newborn in the household. Try to let in as much natural daylight as possible, but at night, softer, diffused lighting is easier on the eyes and more soothing. Floor lamps with swivel heads can cast a light upward and illuminate the entire room or can point down for reading. Clip-on desk lamps and other smaller task lights are also convenient, and can be moved easily and attached to almost any surface. Use energy-saving bulbs with the appropriate wattage. If you're feeling festive, you can add white Christmas lights that cast a lovely soft glow. Battery-operated children's night-lights not only welcome kids into a room but also add a gentle spot of light.

Most importantly, lamps are electric devices, so safety precautions should be considered in a kid-friendly home. Avoid plastic or halogen lamps. Both can get very hot to the touch and may cause serious burns. Cover all wall sockets with safety plugs when not in use to eliminate temptation, and clip loose cords to the wall, too. Anything hanging is a potential hazard.

Choose your lighting with caution and keep the safety of your children in mind. Assess the entire room when thinking about how to achieve a bright room overall, without shady spots or dark corners. Check for wattage and power, too, and try to buy the most efficient bulbs available. With these rules in mind, your home will be light, bright, and safe for all members of the household, not just in the office but throughout the house, as well.

LIGHTING 101

- Cast bright lights everywhere for an optimal working environment that won't strain your eyes.
- Get rid of shady corners; every spot needs light!
- Rely on swivel and clip-on lamps for versatility and convenience.
- Install three-way bulbs to adjust a lamp's brightness.
- Keep safety in mind. Don't use ultra-hot halogen lamps or malleable plastic.
- Cover all open light sockets, and tape down or hide any loose cords.

OPPOSITE Placing an office desk against a wall creates the illusion of a partitioned space, especially with an entire wall devoted to shelving. Add a fluffy shag rug for comfort, as well as a pair of chairs and a low table for another work space.

study/library

If you don't work from home, and a desk in the bedroom or kitchen is sufficient for your household paperwork, but you'd still like a space for quiet reading and reflection, just omit the office furniture and turn your extra room into a study or library. If that notion conjures up only images of dark, oak-paneled walls that reek of cigar smoke, think again. The studies and libraries of today have shaken off their dowdy image and can be designed with bright walls and exciting color combinations. If you find the look of floor-to-ceiling wooden bookcases too heavy, paint your shelves white or swap them for glass for a lighter, more ethereal look. Leather-upholstered club chairs not your thing? Cover the seating with dainty stripes or a cheery flower print. A feminine touch will always imbue a room with style. A spacious and light library can easily be a book-filled haven.

Without a desk and office chair, without file cabinets or the electronic equipment that goes along with a home office, there's room to spare in a study that's used more for relaxation than for work. However, it's still important for furniture to be comfortable. Think roomy reading chairs and sofas, or even a cushioned window seat for lounging. And don't forget to add plenty of lighting if you'll be doing lots of reading and working in this room. Three-way bulbs let you adjust lighting to three different levels, which is ideal if you don't have overhead or track lighting. Soft rugs and plenty of cushions and throws add to the comfort level as well. When the throws aren't in use, simply fold them up and store them in a designated area on the bookshelf, along with the extra pillows.

ABOVE A chartreuse-green daybed, which doubles as a sofa and an extra sleeping area, gives the room a color injection in this citrus-toned study. A freestanding bookshelf in another strong color, like this lavender, contrasts nicely and holds books, magazines, and games.

OPPOSITE A touch of leather in the library doesn't necessarily overpower, but use it sparingly as with this 1940s club chair in dark green. Add cushions or throws to soften the overall look. Glass bookshelves will lighten a space while holding your tomes.

convertible spaces

Because the study or office may sometimes moonlight as a guest bedroom or entertaining area, give careful thought to the use of space when designing these double-duty rooms. An office that needs to include both a desk and a pullout sofa, and still manage to convey enough warmth to allow guests to feel comfortable poses a creative challenge. To make the study-cum-guest room feel like a real room and not like a cubicle where you've happened to add a sofa, pay close attention to the details to pull it all together.

Office to Guest Room

One trick is to cover all upholstered furniture in the room in the same fabric, to give a cohesive look to the space. Accents added throughout that project a homey feel are always a welcoming touch. So often rooms that have two purposes lack a distinct personality—and no one wants to sleep in a room that screams "work." Your guests will feel as if they never left their own office behind! Make sure papers and other work materials can be easily stowed away when out-of-towners show up at your door for a visit. Maybe that means storing work materials like pens and pencils in chic leather-wrapped holders that are both visually attractive and serious enough for an office instead of plastic cups. What type of container do you like to look at? Use your creativity. Even glass mason jars (inexpensive and easily found at yard sales) can add a funky touch. If the room has a closet or shelving, be sure to leave some empty space so that guests can hang or store their clothing. And soft carpeting adds comfort for both guests and those who are hard at work in the home office.

OPPOSITE A home office goes from sterile workspace to cozy anteroom with the addition of feminine floral wallpaper and a smattering of houseplants. A simple desk can easily be cleaned of paperwork so that guests can use it.

STYLE FILE: comfortable nooks

Ever notice how there's always one comfortable corner in a room that people gravitate to? Like anywhere else in the house, such a spot exists in the office or study, and perhaps it's more important here than anywhere else to create a retreat where you can relax for just a few minutes while hard at work. A comfortable armchair to curl up in or a cushioned window seat form the cozy nooks that make a good room a great one.

Consider turning an underused corner into a focal point and favorite lounging space with just a few changes. Add a comfortable, good-looking chair in an eye-catching fabric. Stripes, checks, and plaids will do the trick. Think about the details that add comfort. Include a footrest, a table you can place a drink on, and a lamp for reading. Have a few cushions and a soft blanket at hand, and add tailored curtains in a colorful, textured fabric to cut glare and bring a sense of privacy. It will make the space one you can daydream in for hours on end. A window seat with matching cushions and curtains can make an irresistible space, especially for younger children who love constructing forts. Hanging children's artwork on the walls make a space feel loving, cheerful, and inviting to the whole family. A small throw rug or carpet keeps feet warm and adds a cozy feeling. Or, pair a low table with a couple of chairs in a corner, away from the desk, for sitting with family members or for sitting by yourself in solitary reflection, in a slight change of environment.

CREATING A NOOK

- Comfortable furniture is a must! Invest in an oversize chair or a padded cushion.

- Add to the comfort level with cushions and throws in soft fabrics.

- Cheer up a corner with bright fabrics. Then cover the furniture, curtains, and other accessories with the same pattern.

- Don't neglect the walls. Artwork, photographs, or message boards are ideal in a nook.

- Convert an unused ledge into a window seat with a thick cushion for reading or daydreaming.

- Place a low table and chairs in a corner to add a spot to socialize or for informal work.

OPPOSITE An oversize wing chair in a nook makes all the difference. Cover it in a fabric like this cheery plaid, and add touches like dried flowers and a flowered lampshade to beautify your space without cluttering the desk.

ABOVE Even a nearly bare room can be a comfortable space. A bright, sunny room with clean, hardwood floors lures household denizens as easily as the most cushioned and tailored window seat.

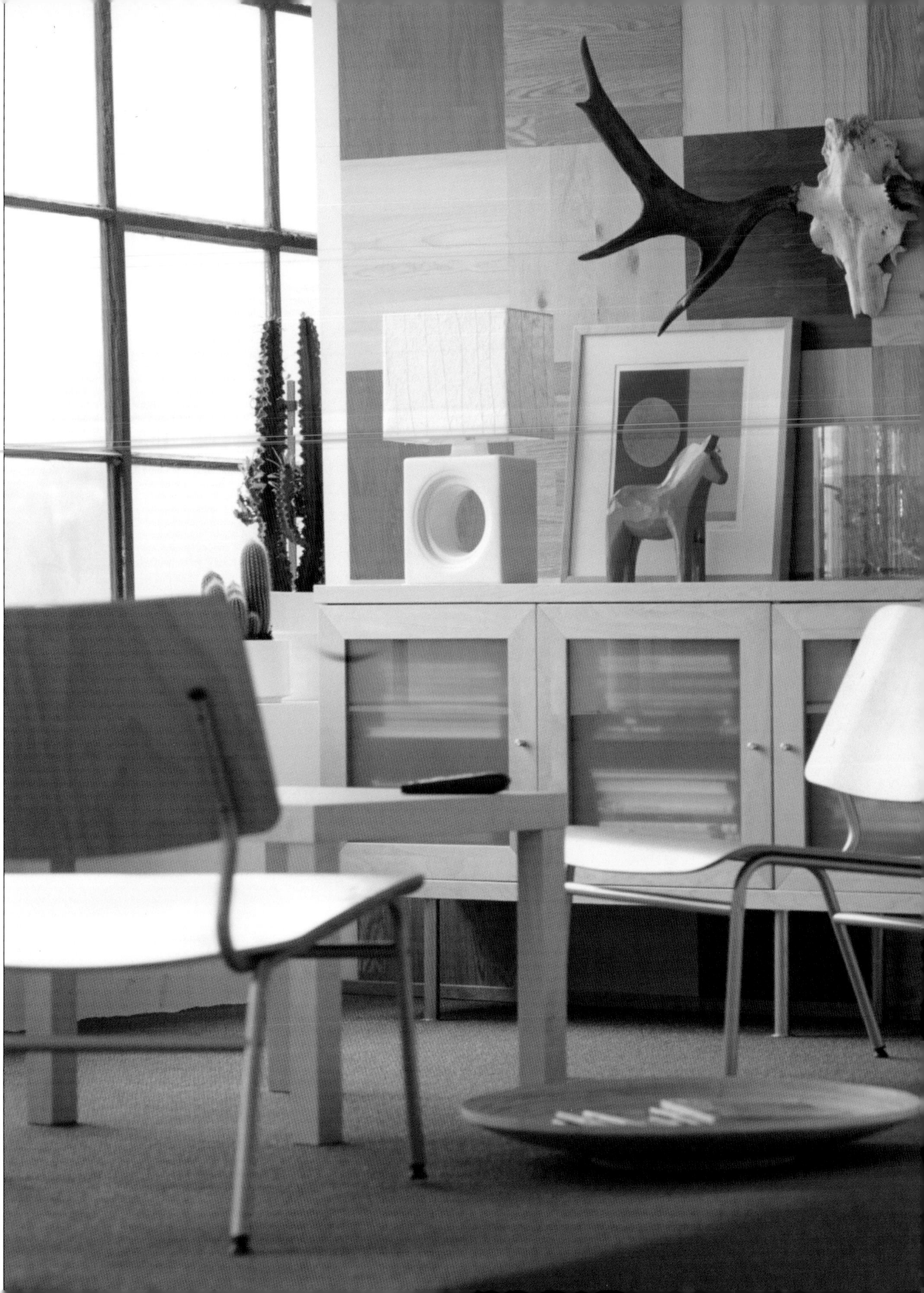

Office to Party Central

Even if your home office is being used as an occasional entertaining space rather than a sometime sleeping area, the same decorating rules apply. Make sure there's plenty of storage for when the room is used as an entertainment space so you can whisk important and unsightly papers out of sight. File cabinets, armoires, and boxes should do the trick. If you must keep certain supplies or tools out in the open or hung on a wall, think of them as artwork: Arrange them in the most aesthetically pleasing way possible. You'll be surprised how pretty your everyday objects can look. Pencils stored in miniature aluminum cans or world maps hung on the wall can create a stylish backdrop. But it's still important to personalize. A photograph or beautiful, small sculpture always has an appeal in a room, and you can intersperse such things with pencil jars and other utilitarian objects for a truly artful look. Look for objects like design-friendly metal wastebaskets and other office accessories that don't compromise style.

OPPOSITE Clear the usual clutter off a console table in the office to use it as a bar or buffet table for entertaining. Plenty of seating and a versatile table can serve dual purposes equally well.

6 PRIVATE spaces

Beautiful boudoirs don't have to be the pristine rooms of yore. A perfect-looking bedroom in a home is an antiquated notion. Children should be welcome in any room—including the parents' bedroom. Unfussy and comfortable master bedrooms, as well as comfort in the kids' rooms, should reign in a household. Think large, comfortable beds, simple linens, and soft flooring. Let the master bedroom's decor trickle down to the rest of the sleeping havens. For shared bedrooms (including those in vacation homes), an egalitarian attitude that's equally low-maintenance but still scores points in the style department shouldn't be forgotten.

OPPOSITE Soft, wall-to-wall carpeting and a big, luxurious bed make this serene bedroom inviting to all. The low height and lack of a footboard keeps the bed easy for everyone to climb into!

a room of
one's own

Bedrooms are like sanctuaries. Everyone needs a private space to retreat to, whether you're heading to sleep or just for a brief time out. As your children get older and become more independent, their need for self-expression and private time emerges. Just like you, they need a space to call their own, where they'll be able to daydream, do homework, sleep peacefully, and have a bit of private time.

Children want to mark their own territory as their personalities become increasingly pronounced. Look inside any 13-year-old's school locker, and you'll find a plethora of snapshots, magazine clippings, sports paraphernalia, and drawings. Kids need to express themselves as their personalities are defined and sharpened, and what better place to do that than their own bedrooms? Try to be lenient with the decoration, and let your child's opinion and taste drive the decisions. They'll feel validated if you take their point of view seriously.

LEFT Although this master bedroom certainly looks grown-up, the cheerful, checked duvet cover, the bright, airy space, and the collection of miniature chairs along the top of the head-board make it an appealing space for children, as well.

A Kid-friendly Master Bedroom

The master bedroom is the domain of the adults of the house, but unless you're vigilant about keeping children out, there will be times, especially when they're small, when it feels like the family bedroom. Enjoy it; they'll be grown and gone before you know it. If you want your children to feel welcome and comfortable in your bedroom, it's easy to choose bedding and furnishings that are washable and sturdy. Keep extra pillows on the bed or close at hand so that you don't have to give up yours when they join you after a 3 A.M. nightmare. A comfortable armchair, especially one big enough for two, will see lots of use if you can fit it in.

Putting a few of their books on the bookshelf along with your own can both provide a distraction as you attempt to get dressed in the morning and makes an impromptu story time easy. Children love to look at photos of themselves "when they were little"—this is a good place to indulge in a few framed baby pictures. And delicate knickknacks and jewelry boxes are better kept on higher shelves or surfaces to keep them safe from inquisitive fingers. Your bedroom should be your peaceful sanctuary, but it will be all the richer for the happy memories created there.

ABOVE Managing to be both energizing and soothing at the same time, this pale-green master bedroom with chartreuse touches is very kid-friendly. Note the extra pillows, the fan placed well out of reach, and the steel and paper lamp that would probably survive being swept off the bedside table by an errant small foot.

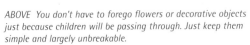

ABOVE You don't have to forego flowers or decorative objects just because children will be passing through. Just keep them simple and largely unbreakable.

ORGANIZING: closets

Making method of a closet's madness shouldn't be such a daunting task. With a level-headed approach, the massive mountain of toys, mittens, sneakers, and clothes that come together in a jumbled mess can be organized into a well-ordered closet space. It's important to teach children at a young age that cleaning up after themselves and organizing their space is invaluable. Their own closets should make this easy by being kid-friendly and easy to navigate. Try not to have out-of-reach shelves or piled-high stacks of boxes. Hang clothing on low, easy-to-reach racks. If needed, a step stool encourages kids to reach for their things on their own.

Add shelves, racks, and hooks at all levels. Several companies make inexpensive closet add-ons, or you can check your neighborhood hardware store. Remember that children's clothing is smaller, so a rack that would have an adult-size suit dragging on the floor can happily hold a young child's clothes with room to spare. Shoe racks on the floor can hold several pairs, and a hanging version frees up valuable floor space. Shelves can hold cubbyholes for hats, gloves, belts, and other accessories. Hooks for coats or anything else should be low on the walls so that your child can easily reach them.

If a closet needs to hold toys, sporting equipment, and other items that can't be stored elsewhere in the room, get some stackable plastic boxes and label them so kids can identify what they're looking for right away, instead of digging through pile after pile. Try to place the boxes in a corner or out of the way of clothing and objects that need to be easy to get to every day. Resist the urge to place heavy or bulky items on high shelves, because they may topple over unexpectedly. Use wood, plastic, or fabric-covered hangers for kids instead of sharp wire. Look for hangers with clips for pants or skirts to hang clothes instead of folding them.

Once your child's closet is outfitted with all its shelving and storage needs, think about adding fun details or exciting colors. Paint the background in a bright yellow that complements the shades in the bedroom, to make your child smile every time the closet doors are opened. Borders that run along the top edge of the closet's walls also give a closet a whimsical touch. Kids may even stop thinking that straightening up the closet is such a drag.

OPPOSITE Closeted doors shouldn't mean forgoing style within. Add artwork like these sweetly feminine drawings, photographs, or a painted border to the wardrobe's interior. Notice the easy-to-reach height of the rack.

personal touches

A room that grows with your children and changes with their maturing personalities can be difficult to achieve while maintaining a budget. And a teen whose rapidly changing whims switch from loving pink one day to insisting on all black the next can't always be accommodated. Try to start with a few classic pieces that you both won't tire of quickly. A sleigh bed, a streamlined wooden vanity, or even an antique needlepoint rug can become a bedroom's core piece. Even family antiques can have a place in a child's bedroom and still last through the years. The heirloom cradle that your child quickly outgrew can become a favorite storage bin for stuffed animals. Bedding, curtain fabrics, area rugs, chairs, and wall hangings are easy to switch and can drastically alter the feel of a room.

A little self-expression is a good thing when it comes to your children's bedroom. Present them with choices so that they'll have ownership of their room. You can even let them have a go at decorating, within reason. Give them a vote in color schemes, fabric patterns, and furniture. Let your children express themselves in the details, and don't be afraid to let them have a little fun. Whimsical wallpaper and prints can fly in a child's bedroom where they wouldn't in the rest of the house. Let imagination run a little wild.

Wall Coverings

Start with the backdrop. The choices for wall coverings are endless, from simple, solid pastel paints to two-toned stripes to lively patterned wallpaper. If you pick something other than a solid color, make sure it can easily be altered if you or your child tire of its look. Hand-painted murals or patterned walls, for example, are difficult to paint over, and require several coats of thick paint. Wallpaper, although slightly more time-consuming to apply (you may want to hire a professional), can be stripped off and recovered. Try to stick to flat surfaces—grass or raffia walls may be fashionable and stylish, but they'll work better in a living room than a child's room.

Floor Coverings

Floor coverings should be given plenty of attention, as well. They can be painted, left untouched, or covered with carpeting. Although hardwood floors are beautiful and easy to maintain throughout the rest of the house, bare wood floors aren't very comfortable in a bedroom. Much play takes place on a child's bedroom floor, and slippery and hard surfaces can become a danger zone for younger children. Soft area rugs that are stain resistant or easily cleaned are a good choice. Pastel dhurries and rag rugs can work well with softer color schemes, and a bound carpet in a bold color can add a jolt of bright color and be a great place to flop for play.

Bed Coverings

Details are often what make a room unique and truly give your children a chance for self-expression. Their bedding is something that's as personal as the clothing they wear—and it's easy to give them the final choice. Fun designs for children's sheets have proliferated. In fact, many companies have bedding collections intended especially for children. Try department stores or mass retailers. You can never go wrong with classic monogrammed sheets, either. Most department stores will emblazon initials onto bedding for little cost, as will myriad catalog companies.

For matching details, look for fabrics that complement each other. Curtains and cushions don't have to be a perfect match, and they can always be replaced if the decor changes. Look for ways to let your children contribute their creativity. They can make a set of fabric- or paint-covered boxes in whatever shade they want. (This can be the place to let them include their latest favorite logos or characters.) Or let them have a bulletin board or art wall of their own design where they can pin things up to their heart's desire. That way, they'll always feel like their room is their own.

LEFT Your kids are sure to love these statement-making Marimekko bright stripes and bold flower prints splashed across their room. The Kukkaketo, Olkiraita, Silmu, Talvikki, and Seven Flowers patterns are shown here.

ABOVE A canopy daybed outfitted with hanging toys, puppets, or fabrics like this Anglo-Indian one is so inviting that bedtime will always be welcome. The canopy can always be dismantled if you tire of it.

a growing nursery

Rapidly growing children present a decorating challenge. Pint-size proportions are quickly outgrown as a 2-year-old sprouts into a lanky 12-year-old. Try to create a room that will grow with your child, and seek out furniture that can transform and change, too. A bunk bed that convert into twin beds, a trundle bed that converts to extra storage, or a changing table that becomes a regular dresser can save space as well as money, and are wonderful pieces of furniture for growing children.

Keep It Simple

In a nursery, furnishings must be versatile enough to keep up with the rate of growth. A crib is quickly replaced with a child-size junior bed, which in turn is substituted by a full-size adult one. How do you accommodate a room whose furniture changes at the blink of an eye? Keep it simple, relaxed, and easily alterable.

If you're converting a spare room into a nursery and don't know the coming baby's sex, or if you're planning to use the room as a nursery for every subsequent member of your expanding clan, it's best to keep the main features neutral. White or neutral shades of wood and creamy-colored linens are the way to go. You can still use color, but do so sparingly and don't make it gender-specific. Primary colors are also a great backdrop. At first babies see black and white best, and then they see bright primary colors. Any shade of red, blue, or yellow is stimulating to an infant and is child-friendly enough to change later into either a girl's or boy's bedroom. Look for cribs that convert into junior beds, by removing the side rails, adding extensions, and adjusting the height. And when your toddler outgrows that bed, it can be used as a small sofa or daybed.

OPPOSITE A romantic crib can beautify a nursery without making it stuffy. Cover walls with neutral shades like these so that a nursery can transform into a child's bedroom or a grown-up sitting area.

Remember to Think Long Term

If the nursery has already been designated to grow along with your newborn, you can add some flavor. A girl's room can be covered in feminine wallpaper, and a boy's room can be done up in stripes. Think long term, though. Will a 10-year-old be just as comfortable with their nursery room's wallpaper? Decorate so that once the crib is dismantled, the nursery can grow with its occupant. Bunnies and ducks are cute, but even a 4-year-old will think that they're too infantile after awhile. Add touches like nursery-book illustrations on the walls, or shelves stocked with toys to announce that it's a baby's room. If you really don't like anything too cutesy, try brightly colored prints by artists such as Miró or Matisse, which can look great in a child's room.

Decorate for the Parents, Too

Make sure the nursery has at least one comfortable armchair. Parents will spend just as much time in this room as a newborn, and it's important to have a chair to sink into, whether it's for the 2 A.M. feeding or the 150th reading of *Good Night Moon*. A sofa or armchair with comfortable blankets at hand will do the trick. Shelves with baskets are a good way to keep clean towels, diapers, and other essentials at the ready in the nursery. Fabric-lined wicker keeps linens dry and clean. Also, don't forget a hamper for wet towels and clothes, a sturdy changing table, and a trash basket for easy disposal.

STYLE FILE: creative expression

Whether sleeping, doing homework, or simply relaxing, children should feel that their room reflects their true self. Let your children express themselves. If they can't find sheets in the exact purple they want, give them a set of white-jersey sheets and let them try to get it right with dye. Better yet, let them create their own sheets with fabric paint or tie-dye. Perhaps they'll want their friends to sign their sheets in color markers. Anything goes.

Another way to let creativity reign is by creating an art wall or board. Buy standard corkboard or a premade bulletin board from a supply store. Help children cover it with fabric, paint the border, add a ribbon detail, and cover it with a collage of ticket stubs, artwork, or photographs. Let them imbue it with their own style and interests, whether their mania is sports, animals, or skateboarding. Display the board above a desk or work area so that their own creativity can inspire them. A pretty option is to crisscross the board with ribbons so that pictures and reminders can be tucked underneath. An art wall is also a possibility. Hang drawings not just on the refrigerator door but in the bedroom as well. Standard art paper–sized frames can be bought at framing stores. Buy a number of frames and hang them together to create a rotating art gallery of your child's work. Children are proud to see their artwork on display.

Even in the most tailored of rooms, the tiniest details that children contribute will give any room flair and a sense of individual style. Always make an allowance for a creative touch that comes from your child.

EXPRESS YOURSELF

- Give your child a blank canvas in some shape or form for self-expression.
- Allow your child to make something for his or her room—for example, a drawing or some other artwork.
- A room should reflect a child's interests; add personal touches like equestrian prints or sports memorabilia.
- Encourage your child to hang photographs or artwork on a message board.
- Make an art wall that's entirely your child's domain.
- Even toddlers are creative; hang their drawings in their rooms, too.

girls' bedrooms

Coordinating chintz fabrics? Floor-to-ceiling toile? Decoration in your daughter's bedroom doesn't have to be limited to arch-feminine choices. Whether dainty or tomboyish, every girl has an opinion on her surroundings and it won't necessarily mesh with yours. Take the time to listen to your daughter's desires before outfitting her room in all pink. Let her make choices regarding color and bedding. Maybe graphic stripes or a windowpane check suit her better, with feminine touches in smaller doses. Or maybe she feels more at ease with soft-green or blue-painted walls instead of classic pink. If her choices are traditional, that's fine, too. She should feel comfortable in her own space. Encourage her to develop her own style, but try to stay away from ultra-trendy choices that she'll outgrow practically overnight.

Although the wisest big-furniture purchases are the ones that work long term, you can have fun with smaller pieces, like bedside tables or benches. They don't have to match; just make sure that they're the right height for the child's bed and that they have enough surface area for a reading lamp, clock, and books for nighttime stories.

Combine the Bedroom and Playroom

If the bedroom will double as a play area, reserve space on the bookshelves or in a corner of the room for doll furniture, stuffed animals, or even a small, child-size table and chairs for playtime. These can easily be replaced with a desk and chair as your daughter enters school and outgrows them. Bins for toys and other objects are a good way to organize, and can be stacked in a closet or a quiet corner. A colorful trunk can serve both as a storage unit and a low bench. Paint it a fun color, and top it off with a removable cushion to make it fit into the room's color scheme.

Hang framed museum prints or other artwork on the walls, or prop them up on bracketed shelves. You can even make an educational trip to a local museum to let your daughter pick out her favorite artwork. Prints are an inexpensive way to decorate, adding tons of style that can please you both and can help promote an appreciation of art at the same time. An oversize bulletin board with a frame-style border is another way to provide space for her to pin up magazine clippings along with her favorite photographs and memorabilia.

OPPOSITE Lavender gets an ultracool update in this girl's bedroom. Choose a classic-white bed frame and nightstand for furniture that will still look great with any color scheme if the occupant decides she isn't into lavender anymore and wants to redecorate. The bank of pillows makes the bed a comfortable lounging spot.

LEFT A daybed like this iron campaign-style version can moonlight as a child's trundle bed. Paint the walls a color like this peachy pink for an instant dose of femininity, and let your daughter choose her own bedding.

KID-FRIENDLY: wall treatments

PAINT

When it comes time to paint or cover walls in a child's room, so many options are available that it can make your head spin. Paints are offered in various finishes, from flat, the most matte looking, to shiny, high-gloss latex paints with eggshell finishes in between. How do you know what's best for your children? Although they're all safe, paint with the most latex is usually reserved for surfaces other than drywall, because it has a flashier, shinier look. So you might consider sticking to a flat or eggshell finish or to a less-concentrated mix of latex. Make sure the paint you choose is easy to clean, too. Keep in mind that flat paint doesn't clean well. Although it may be preferable aesthetically, smudges and dirty handprints mar matte paint very quickly. The less absorbent the paint, the easier it is to erase dirty handprints, magic markers, and other common mishaps.

Be Careful of Lead Paint

If you're renovating an old house, however, other safety precautions must be observed. Find out whether there is old lead paint already on the walls, possibly under many coats of newer paint. If so, avoid stripping or sanding the walls yourself. Call in qualified deleading experts, and make sure the children stay out of the house until the work is done. Paint dust is a common source of lead poisoning in small children.

BORDERS—WALLPAPERED OR HAND-PAINTED

Wallpaper borders and hand-painted details can add a whimsical or pretty touch in a child's bedroom. Chintz flower borders can be lovely in a girl's room. Or, if you want to indulge in cartoon characters or car motifs in primary colors, a border is delightfully welcome in a nursery or young child's room, and is less overpowering than wallpapering the entire room (as well as easier to re-do when the child has outgrown the style). Keep in mind that when a scratch or an errant crayon marks up a papered wall, there's hardly ever a remedy, whereas painted walls can be repainted or patched up with a touch of extra paint. Hand-painted friezes near the ceiling are out of reach and thus less likely to be sullied when children are at play. Use a stencil if you're doing it yourself, or create your own design that features your child's favorite motif.

Durable, simple, and easy-to-clean should be the mantra for kid-friendly walls. The less fussy your child's walls are, the easier they'll be to maintain.

OPPOSITE Matching fabrics all over the room can be kid-friendly and cohesive, as in the animal-print coverlet, roman shades, and wallpaper border that run riot in this bedroom. Tame prints by using neutral patterns in a different scale and lots of white or neutral colors alongside them.

SURFACE SIMPLICITY

- Pick a paint finish that's easy to clean.

- Test for lead before stripping old paint from walls.

- Add a wallpaper border or hand-painted details for a fun touch.

- Keep some paint close at hand in case touch-ups are needed.

- Stick to simple surfaces for practicality.

boys' bedrooms

The same rules apply in a boy's room. Make an effort to include your son in your decorating decisions, because he may need more coercion. Begin with simple questions, like what his favorite color is. It may range from a nautical blue to a hunter green to a neutral tan, but being asked will make him feel involved. Decorate the room with reminders of his personal pastimes or hobbies. If he's a sports fan, he'll probably delight in sports photographs or drawings hanging on the wall or a framed autograph from a favorite team or game. If he's a budding fishermen, he might enjoy nautical artifacts or maps. Likewise, if he's interested in chess, dinosaurs, or architecture, his room should reflect those interests, not only to enhance the room's personality but also to encourage your child's passions.

Design a Space That Grows with Your Child

Invest in sturdy furniture for growing boys. There may be lots of wear and tear involved for active kids. Bunk beds are always a great option, and they save space. Constructing perpendicular bunks creates a loft area underneath for a desk and bookshelves, too, providing room for a sleepover as well as a cozy space to study. A desk for homework in any child's room is a must. Simply make sure it can accommodate a growing child's height. The accompanying chair should also have adjustable seat and back height. For the play area of a bedroom, plenty of storage space is needed. Whether games and toys are stowed away in a trunk or in boxes stacked in the closet and under the bed, encourage organization whenever possible. If every toy has a prescribed space in the bookshelf, closet, or trunk, picking up becomes much simpler.

Let boys have a hand in do-it-yourself decorating, too. If they want to pass on tie-dyed sheets, let them come up with other ideas. Maybe they'll want to display a collection of model planes, ticket stubs, or hats gathered from vacation spots. Give your child an art wall where his imagination can run wild and he can decorate however he likes, even with artwork done at school.

OPPOSITE Don't consider only dark shades for a boy's room; paint walls a cheery taxicab yellow. Throw in accents like this sports-motif carpet and matching bedding. A loft area doubles the available play space.

shared bedrooms

Cramped space doesn't have to mean scrimping on style. When there aren't enough bedrooms to go around and your children need to double up, an extra dose of attention is needed. Personalizing is extra-important for them to mark their own territory. Create separate havens within the same room by designating at least some part of the room as each child's own space.

Two halves don't necessarily make a whole, though. Avoid a disparate look by giving kids options within a limited range of color and furniture choices. A blue-and-green plaid comforter can coordinate with a solid matching hue on another bed. For a laid-back attitude, mismatched furniture from the same manufacturer fits equally well without the stuffiness of a bedroom set, as long as styles don't clash. Use one similar element—like color, shape, or style—to tie it all together. Or if you'd prefer to have matching bedspreads and furniture, maybe the kids can cast their vote on their bedside table, a lamp, or the artwork above the headboard.

Divide the Space Equally

Space-savvy furniture, like bunk beds or a desk unit that accommodates two, is a valuable asset in a shared bedroom. Lay out the room as symmetrically as possible to avoid quarrels over space with a division in the middle. Back-to-back desks, bookcases, or a small table can mark territory. Designate separate storage areas, like armoires or chests, or divide drawers and closet space evenly in a central storage space. A canopied bed or a mosquito net made out of a lightweight fabric hung from above also creates the illusion of privacy within a shared bedroom. When a child craves alone time, the fabric can be pulled down along the sides.

If a shared bedroom is in a vacation home or weekend house, rules and divisions can be more relaxed. The shorter amount of time spent there reduces potential problems in room sharing. Armoires can be shared and beds interchangeable, although decorative details that give a room its style are just as important.

OPPOSITE Twin beds get a separate-but-equal treatment in
this shared bedroom. Although they share a galvanized metal
bedside table, it has separate drawers, and the wainscoted
ledge allows each inhabitant to personalize her own side by
displaying art.

ABOVE Sleek, modern built-in bunks make great use of
space. Use plenty of soft pillows to ensure comfort when
lounging or reading in bed as well as when sleeping. These
beach house bunks don't need be personalized because their
occupants don't live here full-time, but with pure-white bedding and bright pillows, they're highly inviting.

SHOPPING: beds

BUY STURDY AND SAFE

When you're in the market for that restful place for your kids to lay their heads, versatile and classic beds are ideal. For cribs that transform into junior beds, check out the website www.PoshTots.com for a stylish, kid-size sleigh crib or bed. Bunk beds and trundles can be found virtually anywhere. If you're buying a first junior-size bed, make sure that it isn't too high above the ground and that its sides are high enough to prevent rolling out of bed. You can never be too cautious when it comes to safety, even in the bedroom. If you choose to skip the junior bed and go straight to a twin, temporary railings that prevent roll-outs are sold everywhere kids' furniture is sold. For older children, if bunk beds fit the bill, make sure that ladders and slats are sturdy enough and that the top bunk bed has side rails. Trundle beds are usually outfitted with heavy hardware. Before buying one, make sure that the frame is strong enough to hold a mattress (and to withstand a little bouncing) and that the trundle is easy enough for a child to pull out. Look for other options on trundles, too, like the ability to replace the trundle with storage drawers.

Invest in sturdy and well-designed frames or headboards that will last throughout the years. Children can be active sleepers. Make sure there are no sharp edges or hard surfaces that kids can unknowingly hurt themselves on in the middle of the night. Wood or metal beds are long-lasting choices when made well. If you decide on an iron frame, stock your child's bed with plenty of pillows to prevent his or her head from bumping against the hard metal. For a fantastical child's room, beds shaped like cars, rockets, or boats are a fun option, although these will be outgrown in a few years. Canopy beds, which require high ceilings and a bit more space, are also wonderfully private, especially in a shared bedroom. You can create your own canopy by draping fabric from hooks or a cornice attached to the ceiling. A twin bed in a corner can be curtained off for a similar effect. Another option, if you don't want to invest in an entire bed frame, is to use an upholstered headboard—for example, a simple, rectangular shape covered in fabric like simple duck canvas or more elaborate baroque silhouettes tufted with the fabric of your choice. Headboard slipcovers are particularly versatile, and having a few ready-made ones on hand can provide easy, mood-altering switches.

SELECT THE BEST MATTRESS

A good mattress is just as important as a safe and well-made bed. Always buy the best mattress that you can afford. Bring your children along with you to test out the comfort level. Once you buy one, make sure to rotate it periodically to keep the springs functioning well and flip it from time to time, too.

ABOVE A bed with high sides like this wooden one is an ideal choice for a first bed. The sides prevent a toddler from rolling out, and a high headboard and footboard enclose the bed, making its occupant feel safe and secure.

SWEET DREAMS

- If you're looking for practicality, consider a convertible bed that goes from crib to twin, or a bunk bed that becomes a trundle.

- Test drive beds with any mechanisms like ladders or drawers.

- Always invest in a well-made bed if you're looking for longevity. Sturdy wood or metal are two materials that typically last.

- Avoid sharp corners in a child's bed.

- Use a canopy bed to give your child a little extra privacy.

- Headboards with removable slipcovers are a less-costly alternative to buying a full bed frame, but they're equally stylish.

- Buy the best-quality mattress you can afford.

7 COLORFUL escapes

Although it may have the most comfortably soigné of living rooms, the most flexible of studies, and the most welcoming of bedrooms, a family home gains immeasurably by containing another space that can take on many forms but is best described as a "colorful escape." This space may be a welcoming outdoor sitting area or a room dedicated to toys and games. It may be simply a family room where homework and crafts can be done, or an outdoor area where climbing structures and tire swings rule.

Whatever form it takes, it's a room where fun takes precedence, where you can shed your cares and enjoy family activities without having to accomplish anything. Whatever the uses of your family's play area, this chapter will help you make it a safe haven and outfit it to encourage your child's hobbies and passions.

ABOVE This colorful escape is a beautifully designed urban backyard. Its structure is simple, but the reflecting pool at one side adds intrigue, and the colorful, welcoming furniture and the warm-red wall make the space feel alive. Don't be afraid to use bright colors in outdoor spaces.

family playroom

In many homes, the room most fully dedicated to enjoyment is the children's playroom, but playrooms don't have to be reserved for just children; they can be used and enjoyed by the whole family. Everyone needs a space to let imagination flourish, and it helps if children, especially, have a domain where adult rules are more relaxed, where mess is tolerated (for a while), and where the physical-activity quotient can be higher. Decorate accordingly, and listen to your children's opinions even more attentively. Hang their artwork and projects on the wall; paint the room a bright, kid-friendly color; and add a whimsical detail that you know your children will enjoy. Above all, make sure it's a safe, comfortable area where children can entertain themselves for hours on end and develop their creativity to the utmost degree, without too much supervision or instruction.

Depending on your family's interests and hobbies, the play space can be used for any sort of activity. Make it a music room where the piano or other instruments are kept and played, or an arts-and-crafts center where children can paint and construct and where school projects can be completed. It can be simply a comfortable room where both children and adults can read, relax, play board games, or daydream. If you have teenagers, add a pool table or video games for a relaxing environment where they can stretch out, make some noise, and indulge their interests without disrupting activity elsewhere in the house. A small refrigerator stocked with cold drinks and snacks will further enhance the feeling that it's their own haven.

Converted basements, attics, unused garages (if you're lucky to have ample space), extra rooms adjoining children's bedrooms, or other little-used parts of the house are ideal for playrooms. If you're renovating by yourself, make sure that the room is properly insulated and that safety precautions are considered in your plans. Throw soft rugs on hardwood flooring for comfort if you forego wall-to-wall carpeting. Plenty of comfortable seating is important, too, and keep a large area of the room clear for playing. A low, child-size table is ideal for creating artwork and other creative projects. In warm climates, a part of the backyard lawn will work for a playtime space with a climbing structure, sandbox, and a table and chairs in an outdoor covered area. A play space should grow with your children, too: a playroom full of toy cars and dolls needs to translate into a lounging area with a television set and a couple of couches when your children approach adolescence or enter high school.

OPPOSITE Even if a space isn't solely dedicated to playing, fun touches like this sail fan, oversize fish lure, and surfboard bring to mind leisure activities and provide a reminder of escape from everyday life.

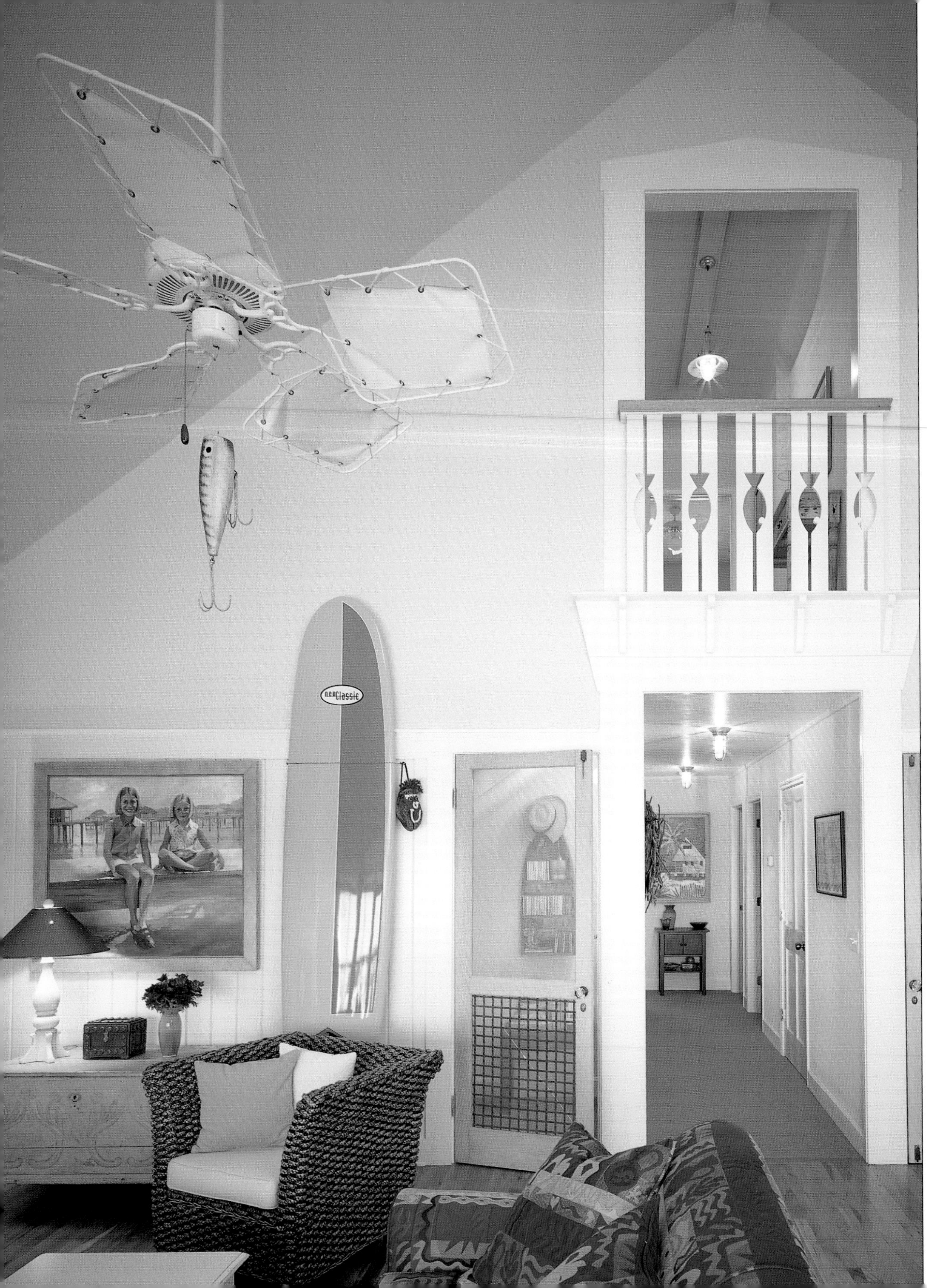
neoClassic

fantasy playroom

Let your children's playroom explode in a riot of color and whimsical details. It can go anywhere your imagination can take you. Do your daughters fancy a ladylike boudoir with books lining the shelves and dainty tables set for tea? Do it up in sweet pastels and soft fabrics. Cover walls and fabrics in pretty patterned wallpaper. But, instead of drowning the room in pink, add a contrasting shade like a mint green or citrus orange for a refreshing alternative. A pattern in small doses can keep things lively—think trim on the molding, carpet, or shades. It gives the room the ultimate ladylike touch for girls who love all things frilled and feminine. Or maybe you have boys who would like their own Amazonian rainforest to romp in. Paint your walls the lush greens and earthy browns of a wild jungle. Add a border of wild animals, or stencil vines on the walls. Make sure to include a space where the boys can build forts or roughhouse. Provide your children with spaces where their imaginations can run wild.

Stencil delicate detailing onto molding for a playful touch. What about a storybook fantasia setting? Cover the walls with scenes from favorite fairy tales and vine details throughout. More so than any other room in the house, the playroom is entirely the children's domain.

Color can add a friendly touch anywhere. Don't be afraid to go big, bold, and bright. A sunshine orange, kelly green, or a piercing violet isn't off-limits here. Go with your instincts and let the rest of the room follow suit. A bright color can be softened by different shades on chairs or a table, for example. Mixing in some touches of white can also provide a lightening effect. Pair stripes or polka dots in varying shades for a youthful look in fabrics and other elements, or even on the walls. Patterns can be just as much fun as a bright, solid color.

Whether bold and bright or soft and feminine, fantasy can mix with pragmatism if you keep practical needs in mind while adding decorative elements. The playroom is a highly trafficked area where kids want free reign; try to accommodate them accordingly. Stain-resistant fabrics, sturdy surfaces, and plenty of comfortable seating can be achieved stylishly, especially if you mix it up with bright colors, plush fabrics, and whimsical details.

LEFT Turn an unused nook into a unique playhouse. This cupboard on a stair landing was transformed into a fantastical play space with some climbing stairs and a lot of imagination.

*ABOVE Transform plain, white columns into a wilderness
fantasy with lifelike renderings of trees for a whimsical
playroom. Cover floors with tiles for a surface where kids
can play without restrictions.*

KID-FRIENDLY: flooring

When it comes time to choose the padding for a playroom's floor, try to combine levity of style with durability and stain resistance. Kids should not only be allowed to be messy here, they also should feel as comfortable flopping down on the floor to read or play as sitting in one of the chairs. No rug burns are allowed!

Assess the needs of your room before making a decision. Is this a family room for relaxing and playing with toys, or will there be messy craft projects taking place? A room reserved for light play and relaxation should have a comfortable and soft rug. Plush, wall-to-wall carpeting is cozy for an indoor play space where little strenuous activity takes place. Soft throw rugs placed around the room will brighten it up and add a soft floor mat where kids can get comfortable. Although sisal, sea grass, and other tough, woven materials are ideal for withstanding dirt and stains in a living room area, they may not be as soft as wool pile or cotton rugs for little ones' hands and feet, especially when playing on the floor. Or, if an easy-to-clean, functional environment is what you and your kids are after, then try wood floors or water-sealed tiles from which spills of paint, glue, and paper scraps can be easily swept or wiped away.

Does your playroom need to suit many types of activities? A multipurpose room can have both a carpeted space for lounging and an uncovered floor surface for messier pursuits. Carpet most of the room and leave a bare-floored area for art projects, or use throw rugs on wood floors that can be cleared away when an unobstructed floor area is needed.

Rugs with patterns and fun designs can also add an interesting element to the floor and will hide dirt and stains better than plain rugs. The playroom is the place where whimsy is allowed. Graphic patterns in funky colors add an edge to a room with a modernist leaning, whereas embroidered, kid-friendly patterns lend a rustic air to a country-style home. Shop around for patterned children's rugs in designs that adults and children alike will enjoy in traditional rectangular shapes and sizes.

FLOOR PLANS

- Think durable, stain-resistant, yet comfortable when shopping for kid-friendly rugs.
- Use tile, linoleum, or wooden flooring in your crafts room; it will make cleanup much easier.
- Combine two types of flooring to accommodate a versatile playroom—tiles on one side and rugs on the other.
- Create a comfort zone with soft, plush carpeting.
- Colorful and wildly-patterned rugs work well in the playroom.

OPPOSITE An open floor plan that contains lots of separate spaces allows your family to enjoy time together, even while pursuing separate activities. The bright colors and the painting warm up the otherwise cool industrial space, and the bare floor leaves space for floor play.

craft room

Do you have an ultra-creative family on your hands? It's wonderful to provide them an outlet for their specialties, and there's no better way to do that than to create a play area where craft and other art supplies are readily accessible and are unlikely to stain or damage anything when in use. In a craft room, cleanup time can be minimized if sinks and sponges are nearby and plenty of labeled storage bins are available. Colored walls and whimsical details can still figure into the design, but avoid overly fragile decorations or furnishings. Surfaces should be bare, resilient, and washable. Tiled or linoleum flooring is best so that paint, crayons, pencils, and glue can't damage them. It's also important that the area is well lit—lots of windows with abundant natural light is ideal. (Although, if your windows face the south or create a glare, you may want to hang adjustable shades on them.)

Purchase some good, working furniture, too, but make sure that it isn't too precious. Plastic tables and chairs that are well made and thick enough can do the trick, though stainless-steel or wood furniture may last longer. A large surface area is a must in the craft room. A long or wide table where kids can spread out their canvases, markers, and scissors is an ideal working area. An old wooden work table can be made even more resilient by attaching linoleum or a thin sheet of metal like zinc to its top. Even a floor stocked with comfortable cushions on which elbows can be propped will do. Easels for a budding painter are a good choice for a craft room. If surfaces are paint resistant and you keep the room well stocked with newspapers, sponges, or paper towels for cleanup, painting mishaps shouldn't be a problem.

Keep the area organized with clear plastic drawers and shelves labeled for convenience. Deep shelves—or even flat file drawers if you have room—are ideal for storing or drying paintings. Kids should keep track of their own supplies and organize them so they know where everything is. Make sure that play spaces for young children have only childproof paints and nonhazardous glues and pastes, too. If you have any doubt about a particular supply, read the label before deciding whether it belongs in your child's craft room.

Once kids enter school, a well-equipped craft room can easily double as a prep space for their science projects and school crafts, but a craft room or an art space doesn't have to be reserved for children. Adults can exercise their creativity there, too. Even if you don't paint or sculpt, a craft room is an ideal place for sewing, making scrapbooks, wrapping presents, constructing models, or, if appropriate provisions are made for tools, woodworking projects as well. Just plan for storage if adult supplies need to be kept apart from children's craft supplies, and make sure the tables and chairs are comfortable for both adults and children.

Finally, why not put up some inspiration? Cover the walls with whatever inspires you—your own or your children's artwork, prints from a museum, or found objects—or put up a large bulletin board, and let the whole family pin it with all of the above, plus cards, photos, and whatever takes their fancy.

STYLE FILE: kids' artwork

Let children sow their creative seeds by giving them the license to create whatever they want in an arts-oriented playroom. Drawing is a relaxing way to wind down and to express complex emotions, no matter what your child's age. Let your children be proud of their creations, too. Hang their artwork up for the whole family and visiting guests to admire. You can frame favorite pieces in ready-made frames. A playroom can even be entirely decorated with only your children's artwork, if just dedicating one wall isn't enough. Watercolor paintings, for example, regardless of your child's skill level, have a beautiful, ethereal look that anyone can enjoy. You don't have to stick to paintings or one-dimensional drawings either. Ceramics, collages, popcorn strung on thread for Christmastime, or any other sort of crafts should find a welcome home here. Think of fun projects that encourage children to decorate their own environment. Painted-glass kits that let kids fashion their own ornaments or decorations can be bought for a rainy day, or a space can be reserved for painting a mural of their own design. Arts and crafts don't have to be costly, either. Found objects make some of the best canvases. Get old bowling pins from a bowling alley, and paint faces and costumes to make "pin people" that will add color and whimsy to the play room. Scraps of felt and unused cloth can be made into puppets, and can also be hung on walls for a decorative touch when not in use. The best way to decorate the playroom or crafts room is by giving kids ownership and letting their handiwork cover the walls, ledges, and bookcases. Not only do they enjoy seeing their work displayed, it also fits right in with the fun, informal aesthetic.

GET CRAFTY

- Get kids into the habit of drawing or painting for a creative and emotional outlet.
- Designate one wall in the playroom as the "art wall," reserved entirely for kids' paintings, or decorate the room entirely with framed favorites.
- Let kids paint a mural on a whole wall or just part of it.
- Decorate with ceramics, pottery, or other decorative objects made at school or at home.
- Plan ahead for a rainy day, and gather materials for art projects.

SHOPPING: tables and chairs

TABLES AND CHAIRS

Tables should withstand years of artwork and play. Placing a table in an unobtrusive corner leaves the center of the room open for activity. It should be sturdy, but not so clunky or heavy that it looks out of place in a playroom. Make sure it's large enough for children to spread out their work. If more temporary table space is needed, use folding card tables made of wood or aluminum that can be stowed away in a closet when not in use.

If the playroom will be used primarily by children, remember to shop with small people in mind. Tables should be low to the ground, and chairs should be sturdy and sized accordingly. Heavy-duty plastic tables and chairs with removable legs are wonderful, small-scale pieces that can be adjusted as kids grow. Beanbags and cubes are wonderfully adaptable to any shape, size, or form of person, but some companies also make child-size upholstered club chairs and rocking chairs. (Keep in mind that beanbag chairs can be dangerous for babies who can't yet lift themselves up.)

For outdoor furniture, note before you buy that the material should be able to withstand the elements. Teak will weather to a beautiful soft gray. Specially coated plastics and metals can stay outdoors without rusting. Look for children's furniture that's meant for indoor as well as outside use, and make sure the material is weather resistant.

SEATING

Because the playroom isn't as formal as the rest of the house, its furnishings can be more flexible. You can decorate it like any room meant for leisure-time use, with comfortable couches, chairs, and lamps for reading. Or you can be more even more informal and decorate the playroom with furniture that is functional but flexible—not disposable, but not investment pieces, either. You can forgo the traditional couch and armchairs and choose colorful beanbags, poufs, or fabric-covered squares. These make great and affordable seating and they withstand active play. What's more, they're also light and moveable enough for kids to clear away or move around the room when they need lots of space to accommodate guests for a sleepover party or afternoon play date. Large floor cushions or futon chairs can also be used for extra seating, adding a comfortable, laid-back touch. Iron-framed butterfly chairs are another option. You can buy different colors and fabrics, ranging from twills to buttery leathers for a more dressed-up approach. Also, look for great fabrics in original prints and patterns.

PLAYROOM PICKS

· Buy at least one table and a few chairs scaled for kids; adult sizes will feel enormous to them.

· Make sure playroom furniture is both practical and playful.

· For comfortable alternative seating, try cushions, beanbags, cubes, and the like.

· Pick sturdy materials like plastic, metal, and painted wood.

· When shopping for outdoor furniture, look for weather-resistant materials.

· Make sure table surfaces accommodate craft work and art projects.

backyard playhouse

Are your living quarters too small for a dedicated playroom? If you have a yard, an outdoor play area can be the answer. Not only does space expand exponentially, but the potential for inadvertent stains on furniture, floors, or walls is gone. You no longer need to patrol vigilantly for markers and paints. Bring on the mud and sand, instead. The only materials that may need concern now are the kids' clothes!

A paved area in the backyard can be used in many ways; it provides an even surface for furniture and a place to play with trucks or jacks on the ground without getting too dirty. A porch or patio with a ceiling is a perfect antidote. Otherwise, flat paving stones, bricks, or oversize cement tiles can also function as flooring for an outdoor play space.

OPPOSITE A solid-wood deck leaves lots of room for all kinds of activities. Sturdy plastic furniture withstands lots of wear and tear, and child-size chairs with ears add a great touch of whimsy. A grassy plot for sports will also get plenty of use.

ABOVE This picnic table provides an inviting spot for family meals alfresco. The bright flowers are welcoming, and the built-in cooking space makes food preparation a breeze.

Unlike the indoor playroom, not much is needed outside. Trade indoor furniture for weather-resistant tables and chairs, and transfer toys outdoors. If you have some comfortable chairs and a few small tables, you may find that on nice days the whole family will sit outside. A sturdy umbrella that won't blow over in a breeze is a bonus when the sun is hot. If you have a lawn and want to encourage the family to congregate there, consider investing in equipment for games like badminton, boccie, croquet, and even Frisbee golf. A sandbox or a swing set is ideal for outdoor play.

Find a place inside where furniture and toys can be stowed away when not in use, or make sure they can stand up to rain and snow. Outdoor storage units can be attractive, and they can also be camouflaged. Water-resistant covers can be bought for some outdoor furniture, or, if you have a covered porch, place furniture there—it will last longer. Even weather-resistant pieces can become discolored when out in the sun. Kids can play on a porch even during inclement weather or when you'd like them to stay out of the sun.

ORGANIZING: storage spaces

A playroom is often a converted garage or porch, or a transformed nook, and consequently doesn't always come outfitted with closets. If yours does, count yourself lucky for having a built-in storage space where toys, extra folding furniture, art supplies and tools, and other games can be stored. If your playroom doesn't have a closet, an arrangement of boxes, shelves, and other creative solutions can serve.

To keep toys and supplies under control, you'll need a lot of separate storage boxes or drawers. Objects like markers, crayons, blocks, toy cars, plastic farm animals, building toys, and many smaller items need storage boxes of their own because they become difficult to play with if they're mixed in with other toys in a large toy box. Kids can't use them if they can't find them. The boxes can be stacked on shelves with toys, video games, CDs, and books. You can also use clear-plastic bins for larger toys and stuffed animals so that when they aren't in use, they can still be clearly visible and easily found when wanted. Bookcases can also hold objects or boxes without obscuring them from sight.

For the playroom with lots of arts-and-crafts activity, a closet can help, but so can tabletop trays or bins to hold markers, pencils, scissors, paintbrushes, and messy paint tubes and jars. Markers or crayons can also be stashed in pencil cups, mason jars, or funky cans or boxes.

If there's a television, stereo, or video game system in the playroom, that means the accompanying videos, CDs, and game cartridges are also nearby. A video- or CD-storage unit nearby keeps these organized, as will bookshelves or a chest of drawers.

SUPPLY CLOSET

- Use plastic bins, drawers, and boxes to store larger items that you'd still like to keep visible.
- Store items in étagères, shelves, or bookcases for easy access.
- Organize smaller art supplies in trays, cups, and jars so that messy paints are stored separately.
- Label supplies so that kids know where they are.
- Keep CDs, videos, DVDs, and video games in storage units specifically designed to accommodate them.

OPPOSITE An enclosed patio space is great fun for toddlers to explore. The table with benches provides comfortable seating, and the statue livens up the space.

conclusion

Today's families are a discerning bunch whose lives are fast paced, multifaceted, and challenging. Most prefer that their home lives be as easy, efficient, and comfortable as possible. Homes must be functional, and once children arrive, they serve many more functions than before, but many of us prefer not to give up on style. Welcoming children into a growing household shouldn't be considered the end of civilized living. Rather, let them help you expand your style vocabulary.

Begin with childproofing, like banishing sharp corners, fragile objects on low tables, and slippery floors. Ease into decorating for a home with children in mind by training yourself to view the world from a child's perspective. Avoid dangerous situations before they occur. Work with resilient fabrics that can be machine washed and sturdy furniture that can withstand years of play throughout the house. Comfort should reign supreme. A fluffy, down-filled sofa is a better choice in the long term than a wood-frame, modular bench. Everywhere, from the tiniest of laundry rooms to your children's bedroom to a grand-plan family room, your family should feel welcome throughout the home.

It's one thing to relive the joys of childhood, but don't transform your home into a mishmash of Disney curtains and foam seating. Reserve the most childlike details for a kid's bedroom or play area. But do preserve whimsy and humor in all areas of your home. Lightheartedness is compatible with sophistication. Living with kids doesn't mean getting rid of your prized antique furniture or fabulous flea-market finds. Luxurious items can still exist in your home—just place them carefully and teach children to respect them. Find a way for adult life to coexist with that of your children, and furniture and family alike will find a happy home. Children can live with antique details, even in the bedroom, just as parents can benefit from superorganized children's shelving. You may even pick up a few pointers for organizing your closet or bedroom along the way or discover that an old lamp is recharged with life when placed in a youthful environment. Toys sometimes make their way into the living room, or a muddy hand can accidentally appear on freshly laundered sheets. Children remind us that material possessions should never be taken too seriously.

Be creative and let your children become involved in their own environments as well. Encourage them to express their design ideas and opinions. Growing children, after all, rapidly become teenagers, then adults, and a good home should stretch and alter to fit shifting tastes and sizes. Look at making a new home with children as an adventure. Your home will become an ever-expanding universe that will always continue to surprise and delight, as will the people living with you.

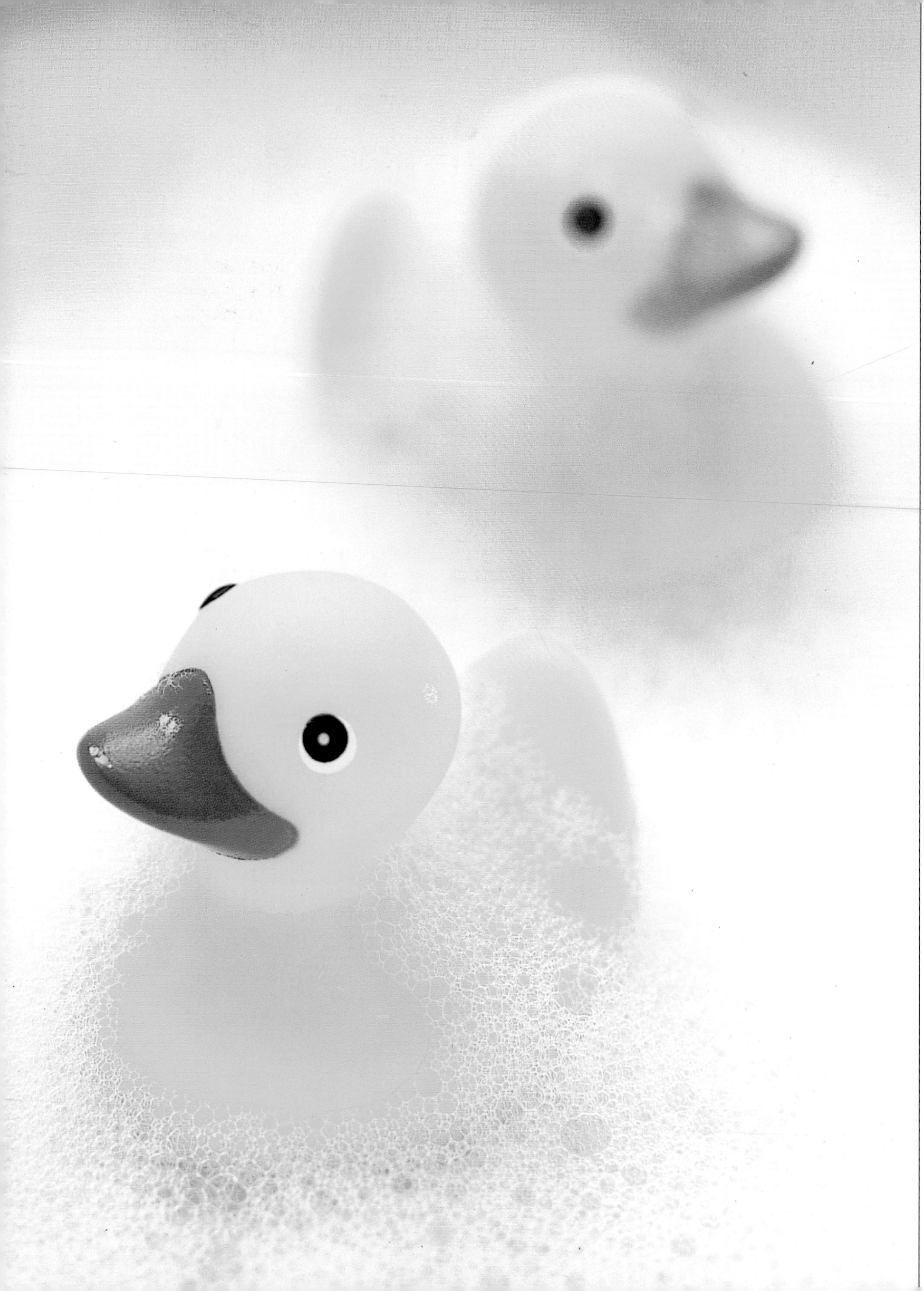